MANAGING
THE EFFECTIVE
PRIMARY SCHOOL

Edited by

Brent Davies and
Linda Ellison

LONGMAN

Published by Longman Information and Reference,
Longman Group Limited 6th Floor, Westgate House, The High,
Harlow, Essex CM20 1YR, England and Associated Companies
throughout the world.

A catalogue record for this book is available from The British
Library

ISBN 0–582–22868–9

Typeset by The Midlands Book Typesetting Company
Printed in Great Britain by Redwood Books, Trowbridge, Wiltshire

Contents

Dedicated to Gib and David and
our friends at the University
of Southern California

List of Contributors

Max Amesbury is headteacher of a large 3 to 11 primary school in Leeds. His early teaching career was in the West Riding. Following an Advanced Diploma in Education at Exeter University, he joined Leeds LEA. He has been an exchange teacher in Australia. In the late 1980s he became headteacher of an inner city primary school before moving to his present school in 1992. He is chair of governors at a local school and has just completed a part-time MSc in Education Management.

Margaret Britton is a primary adviser in North Yorkshire. She has an MSc in Education Management and was previously the head of a primary school on the outskirts of Leeds.

Helen Clayton is headteacher of a 5 to 11 primary school in North Yorkshire and was previously headteacher of a small village school in the Yorkshire Dales. She has a Postgraduate Diploma in Education Management.

Brent Davies is Principal Lecturer in Education Management at Leeds Metropolitan University. Brent is the Course Leader, at Leeds, for an International MBA in Education Management for Leaders of Self-Managing Schools. He is a Visiting Professor at the University of Southern California where he is the co-director of an annual International School Principals' Institute. Brent has lectured and published widely, with six books and over forty articles, on many aspects of self-managing schools in Australia, Canada, the UK and the United States.

Linda Ellison is Principal Lecturer in Education Management at Leeds Metropolitan University and a Visiting Professor at the University of Southern California. She is the Course Leader for the MSc in Education Management at Leeds. She has lectured nationally and internationally on education management and has published a variety of books in this area.

George Holmes is Dean of Management at the University of Humberside and a contributor to the Leeds Metropolitan University MBA in Education Management. His main research interests are in Strategic and Change Management in the field of education. He is currently editor of the journal *Quality Assurance in Education*.

Malcolm Lister is headteacher of a 3 to 11 primary school on the outskirts of Leeds and was previously the headteacher of a junior school. He is particularly interested in the management of staff and his present school is working towards Investors in People accreditation. He has a Certificate in Education Management and is a mentor for newly appointed headteachers. He is a member of the National Steering Group of the Association for the Study of Primary Education.

Allan Osborne is Dean of Programme Quality and Development at Leeds Metropolitan University and is a tutor on education management programmes. He is particularly interested in the development of devolved systems of management within educational institutions.

Jane Startup is the headteacher of a primary school in North Yorkshire and was previously the headteacher of nursery and infants' schools. She is extensively involved in the development of newly appointed headteachers.

Rosemary Thorn is headteacher of a 5 to 11 primary school in Leeds and was previously the head of a First School in Bradford. She has a Certificate in Education Management and an MSc in Education Management from Leeds Metropolitan University.

Preface

This book is written by experienced headteachers and by education management lecturers who work exclusively on management development for self-managing schools. It aims to provide insights into key areas of school management in order to assist those who will lead the primary schools of the future.

Chapter 1 reviews the current context and the management issues facing primary schools. In order to develop a strategic perspective to analyse the broad issues in education management, Chapter 2 establishes a basic understanding of the nature of strategic management. This chapter does not take the traditional school development planning approach but uses the concepts from business to enable the reader to re-think how a strategic management process can be established. Once this framework has been established the book takes six key areas of school management in the primary school:

- creating an effective educational vision;
- management of the primary curriculum;
- managing staff;
- managing the boundaries — the school and the wider system;
- managing the budget;
- managing evaluation.

In each of these areas a headteacher of a primary school explains how she or he manages the challenge that these critical areas of school management pose. Having established personal accounts of how the primary headteachers manage these challenges we hope that readers will draw from the wealth of experience outlined to reflect on their own practice.

However, the good practice of today may not be the good practice of the future. So what are the trends and changes impacting on the educational world that will make significant differences by the year 2000? In the final chapter the author engages in a review of current national and international trends in the economy, education and the nature of management that will change the nature of primary schools and the way in which they are managed. A little crystal ball gazing may provide practical insights to deal with the growing challenge of the next millennium.

1 The current educational context

Linda Ellison

What is the real situation in primary schools today and what are the challenges that they face? Do we have an effective curriculum and high quality leadership and management or are we lurching from one crisis to another with the result that the pupils suffer? Certainly good schools abound, as does good practice within schools but, at the same time, the rapid nature of change is causing problems for staff and governors as they try to cope with the many demands put upon them. There is a need to be positive about the situation if we are to survive the traumas and turmoil which are still to come. We might begin by being realistic and pragmatic about our current situation. Only then can we face the future confidently and positively by determinedly planning for it. We need to have in place a variety of strategies that will provide us with the means to cope with the pressures and assuredly to exploit the opportunities that will undoubtedly arise.

This introductory chapter looks at the current challenges which primary schools face and at the skills which might be needed in order to manage them effectively.

The current context

We live in a turbulent environment but the education system cannot exist in isolation from national changes which are, in turn, directly related to international changes. World trends, such as the importance of South East Asia as a trading area, the increased speed of communication and the changing role of women, have all affected the way in which people think, the nature of industry and employment and the nature of government spending in the western world. Schools are affected in a variety of ways and the situation can, perhaps, best be analysed by using a simple systems model (see Figure 1.1) in which a school takes in *inputs* from the environment, carries out a *process* and then provides the environment with an *output* which, in turn, has an *impact* on that environment.

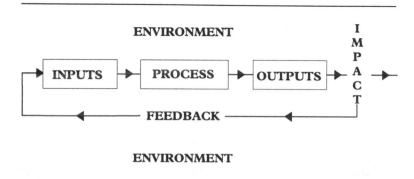

Figure 1.1   The school as a system

Before they received delegated powers under local management of schools (LMS), schools had little control over their inputs such as the way that financial resources were used but they could determine the process i.e. the content and delivery of the curriculum. There was little accountability in terms of the outcomes of the educational process. The position since the Education Reform Act (DES 1988) is that the school can determine the way in which resources are deployed to bring about a fairly tightly controlled curriculum and there is testing and inspection of the outcomes of the educational process, checking that 'value for money' has been achieved, as well as financial auditing to determine legitimacy of spending.

Other factors are beginning to have an impact on this model and to raise further uncertainties. For example, new routes to qualified teacher status (QTS) and the increasing number of mature entrants to the profession provide a more varied input in the area of staffing resources. This affects the process part of the system because there are different needs in terms of professional development and involvement in decision-making. On the output side, there are increasing sources of accountability in the community as the public

Table 1.1

	Input	Process	Output
Pre 1988	Fixed resources. Pupils from a defined catchment area.	Flexibility of curriculum and teaching and learning approaches	Little accountability at school level. Basic auditing.
Post 1988	Block of money for flexible use. Open enrolment therefore uncertain pupil numbers and income.	National Curriculum.	National testing and assessment, reports, Records of Achievement. Inspection. Auditing.
Other factors	New routes to teaching profession. Opportunities to 'select' pupils for some schools.	Appraisal. Altering of National Curriculum. Debate about effective teaching and learning strategies.	Consumer Charters. Long term future of current inspection process. Need for self/internal evaluation and continuous improvement.

is encouraged, for example, through the various citizens' charters, to demand more information from organisations. The situation is summarised in Table 1.1.

The issues currently facing primary schools will now be considered using this model. Some of these issues are then developed by the authors of the later chapters.

Input issues

The most significant and most valuable 'inputs' to the school are the pupils themselves, around whom the whole educational process is centred. Indeed, they are its very reason for existence and if there are insufficient pupils, the school will cease to exist. The pupils bring with them a variety of experiences and have a very varied range of capabilities. Unlike the entry to a bean-canning process, pupils cannot normally be selected and this has an impact on the design of the 'educational process'. A school may be perceived as having particular strengths for example in music, special needs or even on-site after-school provision! These factors can affect parental choice and alter the school's 'community'. For example, after-school provision could be attractive to parents who are in full-time employment, and would, quite probably, include people from beyond the school's traditional catchment area. This can affect daytime contact with the school but may result in wider networks of support and expertise, for example from employers. If a school wishes to alter its intake, then it needs to look at the educational experience which is being offered.

Under formula funding, the school's financial inputs are determined largely by pupil numbers but this gives considerable unpredictability as numbers can fluctuate with demographic trends and as parents exercise their right to choose a school. Factors affecting the schools' reputation or that of alternative schools may affect the parents in a particular area so that they support the school or, conversely do not send their children. It becomes difficult to predict the number of pupils in year groups. Gone are the days when pupils came in blocks such as one-form entry which made planning easy for urban schools. Now all schools face uncertain numbers and, a feature of small schools for many years, non-standard year group sizes.

The financial resources for a primary school used to 'arrive' as x teachers, y hours of support and £z capitation with the local education authority (LEA) picking up the bill for premises costs and with other innovations funded if LEA advisers had the money and felt inclined to spend them on the school. This former system which offered considerable protection, especially for small schools, has been replaced with formula funding under local management of schools (LMS) or grant-maintained status (GMS), the true effects of which are only just beginning to be felt. Transitional funding arrangements have now finished and the Government has increased the age-weighted part of the funding formula, thereby reducing the amount available for supporting small schools. One of the benefits of LMS and of the wider availability of government information has been the publication (under Section 42 of The Education Reform Act) of the allocation of funds to the primary and secondary sectors and to education in general. In most areas there has been a collective approach by primary headteachers to pressurising the LEA into altering the weightings so that they are less biased towards pupils of secondary age. The development of the common funding formula for schools is serving to reduce inequalities across LEAs. Nevertheless, the greatest financial problems are in the primary sector which suffers because schools do not have the economies of scale that are present in the secondary schools. This is particularly the case in the smaller schools which are experiencing severe problems as their protection from 'real' costs is removed. The economic state of the nation means that there will be no significant increase in finance for schools in the foreseeable future. There is a need to have a longer-term perspective on financial planning and to consider a wider source of inputs to the school. The first thought here is to mobilise the parents and staff into more fund-raising events but there are many other areas which can be investigated. The letting of the school premises has often proved to be non-viable as expenditure incurred exceeds the income. Some schools have more opportunities than others in this area. Another avenue frequently tried and then abandoned is commercial sponsorship. During an industrial recession, it is necessary to convince possible sponsors of the benefits of being associated with a particular school if support is to be forthcoming. This may take the form of opportunities for free advertising, e.g. at school events or it could be that the school supplies artwork for the commercial sponsor's premises and entertains at its pensioners' Christmas party. It will be necessary for primary schools to look for wider sources of income and of resource inputs such as materials, grants from the DfE, voluntary organisations, Training and Enterprise Councils, the European Union and so on.

The most expensive input to the school is the teaching and support staff which can account for over 80 per cent of a primary school's budget. Given the possible fluctuations in pupil roll and the rapidly changing world in which schools exist, it is important that the staff have the capacity to be used in a flexible way. This may be to do with roles and responsibilities but, in most schools, it also means that some staff are part-time and some are employed on temporary contracts.

Another valuable input to the school is the enthusiasm and commitment of all the stakeholders. It is the responsibility of the school managers to recognise these qualities and to ensure that the processes which take place within the school continue to provide a climate in which these qualities are maintained.

The expectations and values which people bring with them to the school have a key impact on the way in which the school develops. These expectations and values can be quite varied so headteachers need to take account of this form of 'input' and to work with the various stakeholders to achieve a common sense of purpose.

Having considered some of the inputs to a school, it can be seen that there are several key issues which will continue to impact on primary school management and which will influence the educational process. There is a need to be creative about maximising financial inputs and to recognise the diversity of people and talents which are available to the school. The 'process' part of the school system can then be designed to meet local and national needs.

Process issues

In the last few years there have been many changes to the process of teaching and learning and to other activities which take place within a school. These have largely been the result of the implementation of the Education Reform Act (DES 1988) but others have been introduced because of changes in society in general.

Teachers in primary schools have attempted to embrace the National Curriculum as it was originally designed even though some aspects seemed to be too complex or appeared at the wrong stage in a child's development. There is general acceptance that the legislation has brought about some curriculum changes which had already been introduced in the better schools, such as a broader science programme and improved music provision. There is no doubt, however, that the first few years of the National Curriculum have caused considerable stress. This is not only because new skills and subject areas have had to be taught but also because teachers have felt that the imposed nature of the change has challenged and denigrated their existing provision. It is to be hoped that headteachers learn from this experience and ensure that there is full involvement when school-led initiatives are introduced. Various factors now suggest that there will be much less discomfort about curriculum content in the future. The National Curriculum has been 'slimmed down' by the 'Dearing reforms' and teachers can now consolidate their knowledge as no more new areas remain to be introduced.

As the content of the curriculum begins to settle down, primary schools are faced with another challenge: there has been much disquiet, both from the media, from OFSTED and from reports to the DfE, about the quality of teaching and learning. The Secretary of State for Education commissioned a report which was to look at current practice in primary schools. The brief was to review 'available evidence about delivery of education in primary schools' in order to 'make recommendations about curriculum organisation, teaching methods and classroom practice appropriate to the implementation of the National Curriculum particularly in Key Stage 2'. The report, *Curriculum Organisation and Classroom Practice in Primary Schools: A Discussion Paper* (Alexander *et al.* 1992), was produced very quickly and emphasised the importance of the role of the headteacher in managing the school and in influencing the quality of classroom learning. This document (often referred to as the 'Three Wise Men's Report') received a great deal of attention from the media. Recommendations made in the paper were attempts to respond to the remit given to its authors to provide a basis for debate and to prompt a radical re-think about how best to teach children. Publication came at a time when teachers were just managing to cope with the 'here and now' and had little time or energy to take part in the 'radical re-think' envisaged. Some schools have considered the implications of some of the recommendations but in others there has been little real debate about such issues as subject specialism at Key Stage 2 or more effective use of teacher time. There is still work to be done on viewing the curriculum from the child's point of view and focusing on continuity and progression, both within schools and at the point of transfer. An examination of these areas should now form the key challenge for the 'process' debate within primary schools.

There has been much in the media about schools reducing staffing as a result of budget cuts and about the consequent increases in class size. The implication is that this increase represents a 'bad thing'. Undoubtedly there are many cases in which a school has cut staffing reluctantly, but there are examples of schools where the decision about staffing cuts has been a positive one and where more support staff have been employed or more equipment has been bought. While many headteachers still feel that devolution of power to the school level has been the passing down of cuts, others have been very pleased to have the opportunity to match resources and needs more closely. Governors are sometimes asking what appear at first to be rather extreme questions but, when given further consideration, there are a lot of valuable ideas. For example, one primary school governor suggested that all children should sit in the hall and watch a mathematics programme on a particular topic. There are many reasons why this would not be appropriate but many questions spring from it. Could the work of some teachers be videoed for later use by a whole class or by groups? Could this solve some of the problems of very small schools?

Many schools are having to re-think the way in which they meet their obligations to children with special educational needs, both those who are statemented and those who are not. A member of staff with responsibility for special needs or learning support must ensure that the pupils' progress is monitored and that they receive valuable learning experiences. In addition, he/she is also managing (depending on the size of the school) a team of support staff who have had different types of training and who are sometimes in the school for short periods of time. There is a need to ensure that learning support staff feel that they belong to the school, even though the short-term nature of the funding means that they do not normally have permanent contracts. The management of the whole school system and of the communication requirements stemming from DfE legislation require considerable management skill on behalf of the co-ordinator. This is another example of the increased burden which falls on primary teachers who also have a variety of other roles within their schools. While the headteacher needs to ensure that the legal requirements are met, it is important to keep a sense of perspective; time should not be wasted on producing lengthy reports at the expense of focusing on the educational experience.

As a result of major legislative reform (largely the 1988 Education Reform Act but relating to other areas such as health and safety and pay and conditions), there has been an increased need for a wider group of staff to take on management roles at all levels. Some have multiple roles (as described in Chapter 4). Although this altering of the traditional teacher's role involves learning some new skills, many are already in use. One only has to observe the work of a reception class teacher to see excellent skills in time management, resource management, motivation, communication and so on. What needs to be developed is the ability to apply these skills to managing adults who view themselves as autonomous professionals. It is particularly difficult for those with roles that do not have status in terms of responsibility points. For example, a young and relatively inexperienced teacher could be co-ordinating science, a subject which many staff who trained some years ago could find quite problematic.

The statutory introduction of appraisal in maintained schools has had some effects but, in many schools, it is not going to be the process which was envisaged in the late 1980s when the systems were agreed. One of the main advantages seems to be that someone is taking an interest in the work of a particular teacher and listening to his/her development needs. One could argue that, in well managed schools, this would be the case anyway. The problem in the past has been that only the head has had the opportunity to see and give recognition to the work of others whereas, through appraisal, this opportunity is available to a wider range of staff, especially in larger schools. However, schools are finding it to be a very expensive process in terms of the time required and there is now a tendency to look for ways to 'cut corners'. The management challenge is to look for ways to recognise achievement and to encourage further development without undue time costs. If this is to be the work of more than just the head, then non-contact time needs to be spread around the staff. This can allow appraisal-type work to be combined with the appraiser's own staff development, i.e. he/she can see other approaches to the school's tasks while appraising others. The other aspect of appraisal which can have high potential costs is in the resourcing of identified development needs. It is most important that appraisers are clear about what is possible and that they understand the very varied means by which staff development can take place. The information from the appraisal process must be fed into the school development plan in such a way as not to break any confidences yet so as to make a justified bid for resources. When weighing up priorities for staff development, there is a tendency for schools to focus on the urgent issues rather than on the important but, perhaps, longer-term ones. This can have a detrimental effect on the staff's ability to see beyond the immediate and to anticipate the school's future position.

Many primary teachers are conscious of budget constraints and the cost of replacement staff so they attend courses in their own time, e.g. twilight sessions, Saturday mornings or, in the case of award-bearing courses, in the evenings, weekends and holidays. It is important to recognise the way in which such experiences are feeding into the development of the school and are meeting the personal motivation needs of the individual concerned. Too often the school is very negative about staff who attend award-bearing courses, believing that such activity interferes with school work. Much can be gained by the school if the senior managers take an interest in the projects being undertaken and allow the course participant to have access to information within the school.

The role and involvement of support staff is an area which merits increased attention. Schools have realised that these staff are considerably less expensive to employ than qualified teachers. The tasks of the school are being examined critically in terms of achieving them in the most cost effective way. This has usually resulted in an increasing number of support staff and their being appointed to cover a more varied range of duties. It is important to see them as part of the school's staff and to offer them opportunities for appraisal and staff development, involvement in meetings and in the general functioning of the school.

The main difference between the work of a headteacher now and that before the 1990s is, undoubtedly, the management of the delegated budgets and the associated responsibilities for staffing. Although budgetary and staffing powers are delegated to the governors, headteachers are the day-to-day managers and often have considerable powers devolved to them by the governors. To date there has been much 'tinkering' with the premises and staffing elements of the budget. This has frequently been precipitated by budget cuts so that it has been necessary to prune these two major areas of the whole school budget. What is needed is a longer-term plan within which these major decisions can be made otherwise the school could be heading for problems. For example, if the maintenance of the school's fabric is put off now, there will be greater costs to incur in the future. If staff are automatically replaced with someone similar, the salary bill could be impossible to sustain, resulting in redundancies and low staff morale in the future.

A ten-year rolling programme of maintenance needs to be drawn up and its management needs to be delegated to someone other than the headteacher. In small schools this could involve some form of sharing with other schools, part-time work or oversight by a governor or parent with expertise in this area. Similarly, there needs to be a staffing profile towards which the school will move as staff leave. This profile will relate to the roles of the teachers and of the support staff, the relationship between experienced staff and newly qualified ones and so on.

It will be necessary to consult the governors about their desired level of involvement in the school planning and decision-making processes. In many schools there has been confusion about which powers have been delegated to the headteacher by the governors and there has been ill-feeling about documents which are presented to the governors for the first time as 'final draft'. On the other hand, some governing bodies only wish to have a 'rubber-stamping' role. Similarly, the nature of governor involvement with the staff and pupils must be clear to all. Many governors enjoy working in the school with the pupils but there must be clear guidelines about the way in which this interaction is managed.

Most primary schools have seen the value of involving the parents in supporting the pupils' learning. This has taken the form of parents in the classroom, workshops for parents and the encouragement of various forms of shared reading at home. It is important to realise that parents may now wish to have a wider role, for example in the consultations which are part of the school development planning process. They also expect a quick response to their enquiries and to any complaints which they may make. The school must recognise the parents as key clients for the school's services. The information which parents can offer can be a valuable source of data for school improvement. Open systems of communication will be important for the management of the school's reputation. A similar attitude is needed in relation to the pupils' involvement in the operation of the school. They are, after all, the ones who take messages about the school out into the community.

The major challenges that we face within the 'process' area are the management and motivation of the staff so that they are effective in enhancing children's learning and a more creative and long-term approach to planning and to managing the financial resources so that the money is used effectively and efficiently in pursuit of learning. The achievement of both of these goals will require a fundamental re-think about the way in which planning takes place and the way in which pupils can best be helped to learn. This is very threatening to teachers who have invested many years in their current approach to teaching and learning, have had a relatively narrow role within the school and who have always felt that they had a secure job.

Outputs

In the area of 'outputs', the Government is putting a lot of emphasis on the league table approach, whether it be of pupil results, truancy figures or the hours for which a child is taught. This imposed situation is not favoured by the teaching profession, although, when many teachers are asked to produce their own lists of output indicators, they come up with ideas similar to the Government's.

There have been many changes to the processes of assessment and testing in primary school since ERA. The original emphasis seemed to be two-fold: to ensure that teachers taught the National Curriculum and to demonstrate in an objective way the standards achieved by pupils and schools. The arguments against the Government's chosen approach have been rehearsed many times such as its time consuming nature, thus drawing teachers away from the teaching role, the effect of raw score data on the school's morale and on the consumer's choice. It is to be hoped schools can manage the new approaches to assessment so that they can meet the need for accountability but also feed into the development of the learning programmes for pupils.

As schools have delegated budgets, they are accountable for both the effectiveness of their spending (as reviewed in the OFSTED process) and for the legality of that spending through financial auditing. It has emerged, during financial audits, that spending is not always related to plans and that plans are not accurately costed or monitored so that over or underspending occurs as the plans are implemented. The National Audit Office (which audits grant-maintained schools) produces some guidance in this area as it is concerned that schools should make the most effective use of public resources. The Audit Commission also produces guidance on good practice which is circulated to all schools (Audit Commission 1993).

There are many major challenges for schools in the area of their outputs and the impact that they have on society. Valid direct comparisons between schools are almost impossible to make yet,

even those in the teaching profession take some note of some of
the 'output indicators'. There seems to be greatest hope for those
schools that adopt a client-orientated approach and which seek to
solve problems quickly. There is a need constantly to protect the
school's reputation. This can be achieved through having very good
communication systems and through ensuring that those who go
out from the school carry positive messages about it. This theme
is picked up in Chapter 6.

Environment

The school is constantly affected by changes in the local, national
and international environment and it is most important that headteachers have a strategic view of the changes in the outside world.
Such factors are discussed in Chapter 2 in relation to the strategic
planning process. The range of areas which needs to be considered is
very wide. For example, what skills will our pupils need when they
leave school? What type of projects are likely to attract capital grants
in three years time? What is the most feasible way of providing
education in small rural communities? What sort of alliances can be
made with those outside the traditional education system in order to
provide effective education in deprived inner city areas? How can
stronger partnerships be formed with secondary schools which are
to the benefit of all those concerned? What will happen to the initial
training of teachers?

Many would say that the answers to such questions are not
worth considering because the rapid pace of change overtakes any
proposed scenario. We would argue that it is possible to envision
how the alternative scenarios might work out and to consider what
business the school intends to be in in ten years time. Although the
foreground of the picture will change, it is possible to begin to draw
the background now.

The skills needed to operate in this changing environment

If schools are to be effective learning environments as we move
into the next century, headteachers and others who manage in
the schools will need new skills. Most of today's headteachers have
received a lot of professional development in areas of the curriculum
and expected that the role of a head would be that of the curriculum
leader. Since the introduction of LMS and GMS, there has been a

realisation of the changing nature of the role but the shift, to date, has been towards a more administrative role, dealing with financial returns, contracts for grounds maintenance and so on. This must change if schools are to make the best use of inadequate resources and to prepare pupils for the future.

Leadership is concerned with path-finding while management is about path-following. What is needed is a shift towards a greater proportion of the head's role being leadership. The difference between the two roles is articulated by Bennis and Nanus (1985):

> By focusing attention on a vision, the leader operates on
> the emotional and spiritual resources of the organization,
> on its values, commitment, and aspirations. The manager,
> by contrast, operates on the physical resources of the
> organization to earn a living. An excellent manager can
> see to it that work is done productively and efficiently, on
> schedule, and with a high level of quality. It remains for the
> effective leader, however, to help people in the organization
> know pride and satisfaction in their work. Great leaders
> often inspire their followers to high levels of achievement by
> showing then how their work contributes to worthwhile ends.
> It is an emotional appeal to some of the most fundamental
> of human needs – the need to be important, to make a
> difference, to feel useful, to be part of a successful and
> worthwhile enterprise (pp.92–3).

Burns (1978) refers to the need for transformational leadership as opposed to transactional leadership. In the latter the leader has an agreement with members of the organisation, for example, 'in return for teaching this class for a year you will receive a certain level of salary and a certain number of holidays'. In transformational leadership, the leader binds the partners in the school together with a common vision that empowers corporate achievement. The headteacher must be able to work with the school's partners to develop a vision for the school, thus ensuring that there is 'ownership' of the vision. The vision must then be clearly communicated to all so as to gain commitment to it. In order to do this the headteacher must have a clear set of educational values which underpin all action. He/she must keep abreast of both long and short term trends and issues in the local, national and international environment so that the vision can be adjusted as necessary.

It will be necessary to develop a range of networks and relationships which will create opportunities for the school and which will facilitate the gathering of information about trends and opportunities. The skills of communication, which have, in the past, been needed within the close community of the school, will need to be developed with a wider range of people such as contractors, industry and commerce.

With greater powers at the school level, it is necessary to be able to think creatively about ways of achieving desired goals, about the flexible use of resources and about new areas of business which the school might benefit from moving into. This type of approach is discussed in Chapters 2 and 9.

The skills of the change manager which have been developing over the last few years will continue to be important. Being responsive to change does not mean jumping on every bandwagon that comes along and making unnecessary changes. New demands should be considered within the framework of the school's vision and its long term plan. The tremendous number of changes which offer themselves to schools can cause significant problems of over-load and demoralisation. As well as helping the staff to see that change is part of the normal pattern, headteachers need to be able to look at proposed changes and to filter out those which are less pressing or to make compromises on the demands of some initiatives. For example, a headteacher might have delayed the introduction of appraisal because of a major building programme. If a change is felt to be appropriate, then plans can be adjusted to take account of the new development. A significant characteristic is to see change as an opportunity and to recognise that schools are always changing; change is part of the school's response to the world. If there is not change within a school, it will probably not survive for long. Staff must realise that they are always on a journey and that the steady state will never be reached.

Schools are now more complex in nature and have more demands put upon them. If duplication of effort is to be reduced and if genuine continuity and coherence is to be a feature of the curriculum, the teachers must work together co-operatively. The sharing of tasks such as preparing teaching materials can save time, but one of the biggest benefits of a team approach is that the best ideas are pooled and can be improved by the additional contributions from colleagues. In schools where staff still operate as individuals, it is not possible to have effective teams at a stroke. Team building takes time as relationships must be built, a climate of trust needs to develop and a supportive culture must be developed. Individuals need to see that comments offered are done so in order to bring about the best result and that comments are not seen in a negative way as criticism. When something goes wrong, the team must not adopt a blame attitude but must use the experience to seek ways of ensuring that they learn from the experience and that improvements are made.

If people are to work in teams, then there must be time for

this. The constant complaint from primary schools is that there is no non-contact time for teachers. More creative ways of looking at the school day or of looking at the use of staff time can result in some scope for team meetings. If staff are committed to working together, then they will probably be able to produce some creative suggestions about finding the time to meet and to work in each other's classrooms.

One of the reasons for delegating decision-making to the school level is that more effective decisions can be made by those closest to the customer. There is considerable evidence that schools are beginning to prove this to be so, for example by better tailoring of the staffing budget or the maintenance contracts to the needs of the school. It is important to recognise and to develop where necessary the skills of the staff in making decisions that affect them. Staff should be empowered to make decisions but these should be important ones, not those on insignificant issues. Again, the skills of the change manager are needed here. Staff would feel very threatened if too much decision-making power was given to them too quickly as they would feel that they did not have the necessary skills.

As a leader, a headteacher must provide the catalyst for action, must be ready to learn and must encourage the development of all those connected with the school. We hope that the following chapters provide insights into some of these critical areas of school management.

References

Alexander, R., Rose, J. and Woodhead, C. (1992) *Curriculum Organisation and Classroom Practice in Primary Schools: A Discussion Paper* DES.
Audit Commission (1993) *Adding up the sums* HMSO.
Bennis, W. and Nanus, B. (1985) *Leaders*
Burns, J.M. (1978) *Leadership* Harper and Row.
DES (1988) *Education Reform Act* HMSO.

2 Strategic management in primary schools

George Holmes and Brent Davies

Senior staff with whole school management responsibility within the primary sector are facing the challenge and responsibility for the management and development of their schools as self-managing organisations. Within the context of devolved budgets and self-managing status, the need for headteachers and their senior colleagues to think, act and manage 'strategically' is paramount to organisational survival and development.

Traditionally, while senior staff were the leaders of schools in terms of academic development and operational (or day-to-day) management, the need to take an holistic and business-orientated perspective was less important. The concept of self-managing schools creates a variety of exciting opportunities and, perhaps, some daunting threats. The headteacher for the 1990s and beyond will have to be equipped with the knowledge and skills of the commercial chief executive officer as well as those of the traditional leader of the curriculum. This chapter is designed to support the move towards the development of a 'new generation' of heads by providing an introduction to strategic management concepts, tools and techniques borrowed from the traditional domains of industry and commerce.

After initially discussing the nature of strategic management, the authors present a threefold model of strategic management which can be applied to primary schools in order to improve current practice.

The nature of strategic management

Strategic management is traditionally considered to be the scope and responsibility of senior managers within any organisation. These senior managers (in the primary school context this could be the headteacher, the deputy headteacher and the governors) are responsible for developing the overall goals for the school and for ensuring that everyone works towards their achievement. Strategic management is that group of activities which are concerned with:

> the formulation, evaluation, implementation and control of organisational strategies, strategic plans and the goals and objectives they are designed to achieve (Berg 1990).

In practice, the key to successful strategic management within the primary school is the ability of senior managers *to set up the systems and processes* that can be used to:

1. establish overall school goals and objectives;
2. develop, implement and evaluate the strategies and policies required to achieve the goals;
3. develop action plans necessary to achieve the specified goals and objectives.

These activities themselves should be a collaborative whole school effort involving colleagues at all levels. However, one of the key differentiating features in respect of 'strategic' management, *vis à vis* 'management' is the responsibility of senior managers to take a long-term holistic perspective for the school, to analyse its present position, to identify possible options for future development, to choose the relevant option against appropriate criteria and then to devise a practical plan for achieving the direction selected.

It should be stressed that if a strategic plan is to be successfully designed and translated into action, attention must be given to the process by which decisions are made and this necessitates examining the role of the various partners in the school.

In the past, governors and staff have usually operated separately. It is therefore important that the roles of governors and staff are clear and that they do not duplicate each other's activities. The contributions of all these groups need to be integrated in order to focus effort. When discussing the role of the headteacher and governors, guidelines on LMS state that:

the headteacher will have a key role in helping the governing
body to formulate a management plan for the school, and in
securing its implementation with the collective support of the
school's staff (DES 1988).

There is no simple strategy which can be used to determine
levels and patterns of participation and involvement that would be
appropriate for every school; each school must develop its own way
of working. Do governors merely approve the policies that are put
before them or are they involved in some of the initial discussions
which set the parameters for the decision-making process? How is
the changing role of governors being accepted and implemented
within the school? Staff are unlikely to be motivated if they are
simply carrying out instructions rather than developing a sense of
ownership through being involved in the design and generation of
policies within the school.

The headteacher and other members of the senior management
team are at the interface between governors and staff and are the
key players in the design and implementation of the strategic plan.
They have the role of engaging the governors in a strategic dialogue
as to the aims of the school and how, in broad terms, they might
be achieved. This agenda will also provide a list of performance
indicators for the school and its management so that checks can be
made later to see if the objectives have been achieved.

Good management practice would suggest that there should be
considerable staff involvement in the formulation of the strategic
plan. The term 'staff' is used here to include all those who work in
the school, whether in a teaching or a non-teaching capacity. One
of the main reasons for the move to local management of schools
and grant-maintained status is the belief that, when it comes to
decision-making, the closer the decision-maker is to the final client
or customer, the better quality and more appropriate will be the
decision.

The three-stage strategic management model

This section provides a systematic approach which is designed to
help those with strategic management responsibility to identify the
goals of a primary school, determine an appropriate strategic target,
decide upon suitable constraints, and devise a practical plan by
which the goals may be achieved. For the purposes of simplicity
the strategic management process will be broken down into three
key stages as shown in Figure 2.1 — *strategic analysis*, *strategic
choice* and *strategic implementation*.

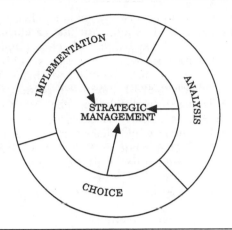

Figure 2.1   The strategic management process

This tripartite method of approaching strategic management is consistent with the business literature, see, for example, Johnson and Scholes (1993), Luffman *et al.* (1991). Each aspect of the three key stages to the strategic management process can be divided into subsections for the purpose of clarification.

Stage one — strategic analysis

The aim of strategic analysis is to form a view of the key influences on the present and future well-being of the school and to appreciate fully the strategic position of the school by understanding how all the stakeholders view the situation which the school faces. These stakeholders include the staff, the governors, the pupils, their parents and interested groups in the community. An essential part of a valid strategic analysis is an understanding by the senior management team of the underlying values, expectations and objectives of the school and of the key influences on it. The strategic analysis of a primary school can be divided into two major sections, an *internal analysis* and an *external analysis*.

1. Internal analysis

The internal analysis examines the core skills and key resources of the school. This would include the physical resources (such as buildings and equipment), the financial resources (the present and future state of its delegated budget) and the human resources (such as teaching and support staff, voluntary help). In addition, a complete internal analysis should include careful consideration of the present service offered by the school to pupils and to the community. The senior management team should devote considerable effort to the internal analysis and should take time to bring together and involve all interested parties and to share perspectives. It is worth remembering that everyone does not see the school in the same way. Headteachers can often become immune to the low quality of their working environment, the motivation levels and effectiveness of their staff and so on, and it is refreshing, if not sometimes a little alarming, to obtain other views from the stakeholders.

A checklist of the key strategic questions to ask could include:

- What is our core activity/business?
- Where are we going at present?
- How successful is the school at meeting its targets/objectives?
- Is the school organisation and management structure appropriate?
- What type of staff do we have in management roles — thinkers, do-ers, leaders, innovators?
- Is the teaching force and management adequately experienced or skilled — for teaching? for managing?
- Do we have the right physical resources?
- What is the financial position?
- Do we have a strategy — what is it (can we state it explicitly), is it appropriate to today — and what about in five years time?
- Are we offering our clients — the pupils, their parents, and the community at large — the right education service?
- How do our clients perceive us?

2. External analysis

External analysis requires a focus on the environment within which the school operates. This can be at two levels, the *macro/national environment*, and the *micro/local environment*.

(i) Macro/national environment

In terms of the national external environment, careful and detailed environmental scanning is needed. Managers involved in the strategic analysis should be prepared to consider political, social, economic, technological and legislative dimensions. Key school stakeholders and managers may form a 'think tank' and engage in a little crystal ball gazing! A useful book in this field is *Education for the Twenty First Century* by Beare and Slaughter (1993).

At the macro or national level, the external environmental analysis would include:

- existing political ideologies and trends in the sector at present, e.g. the move to market competition and the cash-limit approach to public finance; government policy — past, present and future with respect to education, privatisation, and the role of central and local government;
- social changes — such as pressures for a multicultural society and education;
- the economic climate — state of the economy, level of employment, the structure of industry and the demands which these place on schools;
- the state of technological development, its effects on the community, the need to change the learning technology of the school;
- the effects of UK and EC legislation, e.g. employment legislation, health and safety legislation;
- national government legislation and Department for Education regulations on curricular and other school matters.

(ii) Micro/local environment

At the micro or local level, the school management team needs to consider the following in its environmental analysis:

- local trends in employment;
- demographic changes and projected pupil numbers;
- the level of local competition from other primary schools and providers, including the private sector;
- local community needs and client expectations;
- the changing nature of pre-school, secondary and tertiary educational options for pupils and parents.

To enable the headteacher and the senior management team to undertake a full and meaningful strategic analysis and to supplement the descriptive internal and external analyses, a variety of techniques are available, including:

1. SWOT analysis;
2. product portfolio analysis;
3. lifecycle analysis.

Each of these will be examined in turn.

SWOT analysis

This is a much used and corrupted tool originating in strategic marketing and management. Stated simply, the aim of a SWOT analysis is to note down the key Strengths, Weaknesses, Opportunities and Threats experienced at a point in time by a unit or business (in this case a school). When using the technique, it is important that only points of strategic significance to the organisation are noted, and that the SWOT is not used as a dumping ground for a whole list of marginally relevant interesting facts! The SWOT (Figure 2.2) should be designed to list the factors unique to the school, the Strengths, Weaknesses, Opportunities and Threats faced by the school. A good SWOT informs a later stage in the strategic management process, that of strategic choice.

A SWOT analysis is straightforward to carry out because it just involves compiling four lists. It can be undertaken by a variety of people such as teachers, senior managers, support staff, governors, pupils and parents. Figure 2.2 is a typical SWOT form layout that can be used in a school.

Strengths	Weaknesses
Opportunities	Threats

Figure 2.2   The SWOT analysis

Strengths and weaknesses are, as the names suggest, the things which the school possesses which are good or poor (e.g. management, skills, the state of buildings) or which it does well or badly. A possible problem here is that staff may be unwilling to articulate weaknesses if they believe that there is an element of accountability present. Realistic self-evaluation or team evaluation will be minimal in such circumstances. Staff will not be honest about themselves and all weaknesses will be of other areas and activities. They need to feel that there is a sense of trust and that what they say will not be used out of context. It is therefore important to have the right culture and climate before starting a SWOT analysis. Often schools may prefer to use the term 'areas for development' so as to avoid the negative or critical connotations associated with 'weaknesses'.

Opportunities are potential openings which could be grasped in the future. To list the opportunities, it is necessary to have a clear view of the environment in which the school will operate in the medium to long term. Nothing is static; the educational world has changed very radically over the last ten years and probably will continue to do so. There is a need to be creative so a broad perspective is required. Outsiders to the school may provide a different view that will be helpful in determining the likely opportunities that may be presented in the future. With threats as with the identification of possible opportunities, there needs to be some degree of vision about the future educational environment if potential threats to the school or area are to be highlighted in plenty of time so that they can be countered.

If the strategic management process is successful, it will help the school to capitalise on its strengths, overcome its weaknesses, exploit its opportunities and minimise the effect of the threats.

Product portfolio analysis

Two useful models of product portfolio analysis are available from the 'business world' in the form of the Boston Consulting Group Matrix (BCG Matrix) and the General Electric Industrial Attractiveness Matrix (the GE Screen). These are discussed below:

The BCG Matrix The BCG Matrix (see Johnson and Scholes 1993) is designed with four quadrants, the dog, the problem child, the star and the cash cow! The two dimensions to the Matrix are the rate of growth in the market on the one hand, and the market share on the other. This is shown in Figure 2.3.

By using this commercial technique, business organisations consider their product positioning in the market place. It has valuable applicability to schools where either the whole educational process or one part of the school's activity is taken as the 'product'.

A so-called 'dog product' would be identified as being one where the organisation has a low market share in a low growth market. Clearly, this type of product is 'going nowhere' and the organisation would be advised to exit from this particular offering/market. In the educational setting this could be characterised by a failing school

Figure 2.3　The Boston Consulting Group Matrix

with relatively low and declining pupil numbers in a period (or region) of demographic downturn.

The problem child, on the other hand, can be described as a product or activity operating within a high growth market in which the organisation has only a small level of market penetration. This particular quadrant is aptly named as the task of the organisation would be to nurture and carefully develop its market offering in an attempt to gain market share at a later date. This, in the educational context, can be seen as a school located in an area which has a rapidly increasing population but where large numbers of parents are opting to send their children to other schools.

Successful problem children should become 'star' category activities, i.e. those that have a high market share in a fast growing market. Often it is the case that a star product offers the organisation the opportunity to be the market leader. The problem with star offerings, however, is that they require large and continuous investment to enable the organisation to keep pace with the high growth market in order to retain its leadership position. This describes the oversubscribed school in an area where the demographic trends indicate that the pupil roll is growing fast.

This is where the concept of the 'cash cow' comes in. The cash cow is a product or service with which the organisation dominates the market at a time when the market growth rate is slowing or low. With little cash or capital investment required to maintain the market position (given the low growth rate) the organisation has the opportunity to 'milk' this particular activity for cash returns. In an organisation with a balanced portfolio, these revenue streams should, in turn, be used to subsidise and support the 'problem children' and 'stars' of today which should become the cash cows of tomorrow. This would describe a nursery unit with little competition where, because of lack of alternatives, the school takes all the pupils in a fairly static catchment area.

While such a model and its commercial orientation towards market shares and market growth rates may have limitations, it should be possible for the innovative and creative thinking headteacher to consider the variety of activities offered by the school and to place these into the quadrants of the Matrix. What about starting a nursery? Does this have the potential for being a star product or just another problem child? Are school lettings a cash cow or a dog? The reader may wish to consider in his/her own unique context where to put school meals, instrumental lessons, the school tuck shop, after school activities and community use in the quadrants of the Matrix.

The model has two functions if used carefully. It provides an analytical framework for the current mix of activities and it

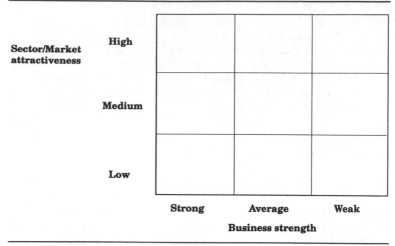

Figure 2.4   General Electric's Industry Attractiveness Matrix

highlights gaps in the types of activity presently undertaken which could determine future options.

The General Electric Screen   The General Electric Screen (see Hofer and Schendel 1978) is a two-dimensional matrix with axes concentrating on sector/market attractiveness and on business strength. This is shown in Figure 2.4. Here managers are asked to consider the present position of their activities in terms of their strength within the marketplace, i.e. strong, average or weak, as plotted against the market attractiveness of the particular market within which they are operating, i.e. low, medium or high.

When interpreting the GE Matrix and putting it to use, it is important to recognise the key descriptors to the axes. Relative business strength could be determined by a number of factors which include:

- relative market share;
- management skills;
- product/service quality;
- reputation;
- location.

Using these descriptors, it is quite possible for a primary school with experienced management, a high quality of education and a good reputation, to describe itself as having a strong business position on the GE Matrix. Those, however, in schools experiencing a low share of available pupil recruitment, a poor image and a bad location would place themselves in one of the 'weak' segments.

If we turn now to the other dimension to the model, measures of sector/market attractiveness, a range of possible descriptors again can be provided:

- market size;
- profit margins;
- competition;
- growth rate;
- supplier power.

In the case of a primary school therefore, a school operating in an area of the country where the demographic trend for those of primary school age is falling and where there is a significant amount of competition from neighbouring schools, could be described as being in the 'low sector' when it comes to market attractiveness. Conversely, a school encountering a demographic boom with little competition and a rapid growth in relocation to the area may wish to describe its market as being highly attractive and in the upper left hand sector of the GE screen.

Clearly, the ideal position for a school within the GE screen would be to find itself in a strong position in terms of relative market share, management skills, product/service quality, reputation and location and in a highly attractive position in terms of market size, competition, growth rate and supplier power. Conversely, a school on the verge of 'failure' may find its positioning to be weak within a low/unattractive market.

Wherever the school (or its constituent activities) finds itself in these matrices, the analysis process provides a valuable method of developing strategies to improve the school's relative strategic position by focusing on sectors of the matrix that can be improved by management action.

The Lifecycle Portfolio Matrix (adapted from Little 1974)

The Lifestyle Portfolio Matrix is a business approach that can readily be transferred to education. The two dimensions of this matrix are shown in Figure 2.5 and are the competitive position of the organisation and the stages of industrial maturity.

As can be seen in Figure 2.5, competitive position is described from dominant through strong, favourable and tenable to weak and the stages of industrial maturity from embryonic through growth, maturity to ageing/decline.

In order to apply the Lifecycle Portfolio Matrix effectively, there is a need for the reader to understand the terms used in respect of the competitive dimension of the Matrix. Little (1974) describes a dominant position within the Matrix as being one of

Stages of Industrial Maturity

Competitive position	Embryonic	Growth	Mature	Ageing
Dominant	Fast grow Start up	Fast grow Attain cost leadership Renew Defend position	Defend position Attain cost leadership Renew Fast grow	Defend position Focus Renew Grow with industry
Strong	Start up Differentiate Fast grow	Fast grow Catch up Attain cost leadership Differentiate	Attain cost leadership Renew, focus Differentiate Grow with industry	Find niche Hold niche Hang-in Grow with industry Harvest
Favourable	Start up Differentiate Focus Fast grow	Differentiate, focus Catch up Grow with industry	Harvest, hang-in Find a niche, hold niche Renew, turnaround Differentiate, focus Grow with industry	Retrench Turnaround
Tenable	Start up Grow with industry Focus	Harvest, catch up Hold niche, hang-in Find niche Turnaround Focus Grow with industry	Harvest Turnaround Find niche Retrench	Divest Retrench
Weak	Find niche Catch up Grow with industry	Turnaround Retrench	Withdraw Divest	Withdraw

Figure 2.5   The Lifecycle Portfolio Matrix (from Little 1974)

monopoly/quasimonopoly in which the individual organisation acts as single supplier to the market (i.e. the only school). The strong position is expressed as one in which the organisation is able to follow its own strategies without reference to the competition (the only school for miles). The favourable position describes an organisation as a market leader (first amongst equals). An example of this would be a school which is historically the best in the district. A tenable position can be maintained by keeping a focus (hard-working local school just hanging in there!) and a weak position means that, for example, a school is probably unable to survive in the long run (such as a very small school).

The 'stages of industrial maturity' dimension to the Matrix is drawn from the discipline of marketing, namely the concept of the product lifecycle, i.e. that all products have four key stages to their development, from embryonic when the product is initially launched, followed by a fast growth phase, culminating in maturity when the product reaches market saturation point and, finally, the ageing phase when the product starts to decline in the market place.

The advantage of this particular tool lies not in the distinctiveness of the analytical framework itself, but in the strategic advice proffered by Little (1974) for organisations or activities positioned within each sector of the matrix. By way of an extreme example, the school finding itself positioned in the lower right-hand sector, i.e. with a weak position in a declining market, would be advised to take the only practicable strategic decision and to withdraw. Those in the upper left-hand position, i.e. dominant schools in new or fast-growing areas/markets would do well to follow the advice of Little (1974) to grow fast, defend their position, and strive to maintain efficient low-cost structures.

This advocacy for strategy based upon an analytical framework provides a logical progression to the next stage of our examination of strategic management, the issue of strategic choice.

Stage two — strategic choice

Having completed a careful and systematic strategic analysis of the school's present position, i.e. the 'where are we now?', the headteacher and her/his team are in a position to begin to consider the future development of the school. This component of the strategic management process is known as strategic choice or the 'where are we going?' element.

In essence, strategic choice involves two key stages. The first is the identification or generation of possible future options for the school, and the second is the evaluation of the options generated against valid criteria in order to make a sound selection of a future direction or strategy. Underlying this process is the concept of a strategic logic, that is the matching of options with the competitive situation and with the relative strategic capabilities of the school.

Strategic options

Let us look first at the generation of potential strategic options. It is relatively easy to draw up, again from the commercial literature, a menu of key strategic options applicable to most organisations which the headteacher and his/her team may tailor to the school's specific needs and situation. Some of the possible strategic options for future development are listed below, with some examples in order to clarify meaning:

- doing nothing (i.e. continuing to follow a successful strategy) — but beware of developments?;
- withdrawal from unsatisfactory or non-compatible areas of the business portfolio, e.g. stop lettings or loss-making extra-curricular music provision?;
- consolidation (growing with the market, or defending the position in a mature market) e.g. go back to quality teaching and learning as a focus after rapid change and reorganisation?;
- market penetration (gaining market share) — market aggressively?;
- product/service development (developing new provision), e.g. provide breakfasts, run an 'after-school club'?;
- market development (entering new segments of the market or geographical areas);
- diversification into;
  (a) related activities — sell education services to adults, e.g. adult literacy classes;
  (b) activities with no clear relationship with existing core business — e.g. hire hall for functions?;
- vertical integration forwards or backwards, e.g. take over a local nursery school, move from infant to infant and junior provision.

Clearly many of the above terms seem initially alien to the primary school environment, but it is possible as was shown with the examples, to consider them in an educational context. Obviously, not all of the potential strategic options will be open to all schools, or indeed desirable to follow. The same holds true as it did for the various matrices offered earlier in this chapter: they provide a new or different way of looking at the strategic development and position of your school.

Strategic evaluation

We move on now to the second stage of the strategic choice process: considering the screening or evaluation of potential strategic options. Basically, we present three key criteria for the evaluation of a strategic option:

- suitability;
- acceptability;
- feasibility.

The headteacher and his/her team should have drawn up a list of possible strategic options or directions appropriate for the school based upon key strengths, weaknesses, opportunities and threats. They should have audited the core skills and key resources presently available, and have taken note of the output of the various processes associated with strategic analysis.

Each option is considered in terms of its suitability, i e the ability of the strategic option to overcome the difficulties identified in the strategic analysis, the potential to exploit strengths and opportunities and to fit with long-term objectives.

The acceptability of an option is determined by balancing such factors as:

- costs;
- risk;
- ability to meet expectations;
- fit with existing structures and systems;
- effect upon groups and individuals.

Finally, the feasibility of the suggested strategy or option is evaluated using the following criteria:

- Can the option or related strategy be funded?
- Can the organisation perform at the desired level?
- How will the organisation secure or develop the necessary skills?
- Can the necessary position be achieved?
- Can competitive reaction to the option or strategy be coped with?

If, on balance, the senior management team feels that the option generated and selected is suitable, acceptable and feasible, it may choose to present the analysis for approval to the governing body (where necessary). Inevitably, this will lead to questions of implementation, i.e. how is the planned direction or change going to be implemented? This brings us to the final component in the triumvirate, strategic implementation.

Stage three — strategic implementation

Of all the components of strategic management, it is the implementation which causes the most difficulty. Taking colleagues with you in the discussion, analysis and planning stages is usually relatively easy as most teachers enjoy the opportunity to contribute, to use their problem-solving skills and to influence developments. The formation of a systematic implementation plan which identifies, prioritises and provides details of the physical, human and financial resource needs is similarly straightforward. Staff rooms and head-teachers' rooms throughout the nation are full of well-intentioned but dusty school development plans as testament to this assertion. However, 'doing the business', and initiating and sustaining planned, systematic and, sometimes, revolutionary change can be a demanding and often impossible task because, as Kanter (1983) suggests, from now on the change is going to affect someone's job!

Resistance to change is a human condition (see Fullan 1991) and the headteacher should be prepared to encounter significant limitations to any strategic development. The keys to successful strategy implementation appear to be:

- careful involvement of key players in all stages of formulation;
- the development of a commitment to making things happen;
- the resources and legitimate authority to (if necessary) break down resistance barriers.

The literature on strategic management from the commercial sector adds the following to these success factors: the need to plan and allocate tasks and priorities; the need to provide a structure which is compatible with the strategy; the need to develop people and systems which embrace change. It is not surprising that many headteachers find this the most challenging stage! A useful account of implementation approaches is provided by Davies and Ellison (1992) in their book *School Development Planning*.

Conclusion

Readers will be familiar with the traditional approach to school development planning as a way of developing an effective planning process for the school. What this chapter has sought to do is to take a business approach to strategic management planning to contrast with that traditional approach. By doing so we hope to develop new perspectives on strategic analysis, choice and implementation that will give the reader different tools to tackle the increasing complexity of school planning. 'Think differently, think strategically' might, we hope, replace the 1970s Californian expression 'think pink'!

References

Beare, H. and Slaughter, R. (1993) *Education for the Twenty First Century* Routledge.

Berg, N.A. (1990) *Strategic Management: Policy and Planning* Harvard Press.

Davies, B. and Ellison, L. (1992) *School Development Planning* Longman.

DES (1988) Education Reform Act: Local Management of Schools, *Circular 7/88* DES.

Fullan, M. (1991) *The New Meaning of Educational Change* Cassell.

Hofer, C. and Schendel, D. (1978) *Strategy Formulation: Analytical Concepts* West Publishing.

Johnson, G. and Scholes, K. (1993) *Exploring Corporate Strategy — Texts and Cases* Prentice Hall.

Kanter, R.M. (1983) *The Change Masters* Routledge.

Little, A. (1974) 'The Lifestyle Portfolio Matrix' in Wright, R.V.L. (ed.) *A System of Managing Diversity* West Publishing.

Luffman, G., Sanderson, S., Lea, E. and Kenny, B. (1991) *Business Policy — An Analytical Introduction* Blackwell Business.

3 Creating an effective vision for a primary school

Helen Clayton

This chapter sets out to examine the elements of an effective vision and mission for a primary school, and the role of leadership needed to develop and deliver it. It also describes the way in which I sought, within a small primary school, to develop a vision and to work towards its achievement.

Bennis and Nanus (1985, p.89) define vision as:

> a mental image of a possible and desirable future state of the organisation . . . as vague as a dream or as precise as a goal or mission statement . . . a view of a realistic, credible, attractive future for the organisation, a condition that is better in some important ways than what now exists.'

The key element that can be drawn from this quotation is that, by looking ahead, it is possible to foresee an attractive and better organisation. The emphasis is on the positive to enable a school to see the excellence which it is capable of achieving and to strive to reach that desired state. Davies and Ellison (1992, p.5) state that vision:

> is the basic purpose and values to which the school aspires and it sets the context for the management of the school's activities.

Here the important elements for me are purpose, values and management. The vision is necessary in order to establish the purpose of the school, to communicate the values which will underpin decision-making and to inform the management strategies which will take the school forward. 'Aspirations for the future' are also found in ideas generated by others, for example:

> The purpose of vision is to help the school move from the known to the unknown; to set out the hopes and aspirations of the school for children, community and staff (West-Burnham 1992, p.103).

Every school depends for its future on having a 'vision', a blueprint of a desired future state, the achievement of which is the aim of everyone connected with the school. This vision needs to incorporate, encapsulate and illuminate all aspects of school life. It should be an effective synthesis of beliefs and ideals, of values and functions, of past achievements and future aspirations, of choices and constraints. Above all the vision should be shared and owned by all concerned with the school and should provide the inspiration and challenge which enables all those people to achieve high levels of self-motivation.

A key phrase is 'shared and owned'. It is important that the headteacher has, for his/her school, an implicit vision which has developed over time in the course of his/her professional development. It will probably have aspects of the three interlinked strands of educational philosophy, of school-centred beliefs and of personal and professional aspirations for self and others. Different individuals and groups connected with the school will also have personal visions of a 'good school', although for some these may seem to be insubstantial, transient and transitory. These personal implicit visions will all be different. They will never be realised as a school vision unless they become fused into an explicit whole school vision which is shared and owned by all: an empowering vision.

At first sight it may seem that the quickest way to establishing a whole school vision would be for the headteacher to articulate his/her personal vision and for this to be accepted as the whole school vision. This would appear to be efficient in terms of time and to be a straightforward process for producing written documentation. However this vision would be ineffective — it would never become a reality, the attainable dream. The only effective vision is the one which places staff at the centre, is truly shared and owned by all. It develops through professional dialogue and debate, through common experiences and practical examples, through the development of participative management processes, through whole-school professional development and, above all, through quality professional and personal relationships based on trust. It is important that the leader believes that the staff can work together to achieve the vision.

In terms of human, financial and time resources the cost of realising a shared, owned, whole-school vision is very high. Indeed there are some who will argue that, in these days of self-management, the school cannot afford it and that the National Curriculum means that every school has the same curriculum to follow and hence has no need for its own vision. The opposite is in fact the truth — for the foreseeable future no school can afford to be without a whole school vision, particularly a curriculum-focused one. The curriculum is the heart of the school and ultimately all schools succeed or fail in terms of the teaching and learning which takes place in them.

A vision is then an ideal which can only be purposed and implemented through a mission, a managerial means of making the vision a reality through example, action, words and documentation. The process by which the vision is articulated and purposed is all important because, while the philosophy and wording of the vision and its documentation may be virtually independent of the process used — indeed it may appear identical for both top-down and bottom-up management styles and processes — it is only the vision achieved through real involvement and meaningful participation which will receive total commitment and thus ensure its translation into meaningful action and common practice.

The process of achieving a shared vision and a participative management style is a critical task which is crucial for the success and well-being of the school. It is, therefore, essential that this task is given the highest priority by the school's management. In his/her leadership role, the headteacher must organise meaning for those connected with the school so that they begin to see what can be achieved and how they can work towards the desired state.

On my arrival at a small village primary school there was no apparent view of the future. After discussion with staff, governors and community leaders, it was obvious that, for three years, the main vision of the future and the focus of all activity had been the continuation of education in the village. The school had been threatened with closure so everyone's efforts had been targeted to enable it to remain open. This battle had been won, the goal had been reached and there the vision ended.

My aim, on taking up the post of headteacher was to involve everyone in decision-making, to give purpose, to establish values and to move forward. The school had ticked over for several years for a variety of reasons. Involvement in the school by outside agencies was minimal, staff morale was low, the curriculum offered to the children was narrow and delivered in a formal manner and the internal school environment was like a desert. The image that I had of the school in the years ahead was a different place. However, I knew that it was necessary to establish ownership of the decisions which would be needed along an incremental path by all those involved. This perspective is outlined by Fullan (1992):

> Schools are not in the business of managing single inno
> vations; they are in the business of contending with multiple
> innovations simultaneously. In such situations a more
> generically powerful approach is needed, namely, helping to
> develop and foster collaborative work cultures.

This encompasses how I felt about the school. There were many innovations needed and others which would be imposed and it was essential that the members of the school worked together. However, my role as the leader was central to the journey which we were to undertake. My task was to get the teachers from where they were at that point to where they had not been! I knew that the staff were stepping into the unknown and that they would need a great deal of support to enable them to take the first step. I had a vision of a better school which would be delivering quality education. My role was as a transformational leader responding to the needs of followers, looking for the potential motives in followers, seeking to satisfy higher needs and engaging the full person.

The staff and children were like coal waiting to be set alight! It was evident to me that the potential was locked up and a key was needed to open the door, to allow the children and staff to reach it. I was aware that the vision needed to be built and that everyone must be involved. My view of leadership is reflected in the quote from West-Burnham (1990, p.70):

> Leadership is about vision, motivating managing teams,
> creating appropriate structures and being as concerned with
> the people as the tasks.

In my role as leader I feel strongly that the people involved in any task are the key to its success. In order to build a vision of the future for our institution we had to move along the road towards it. Initially I took the steps and the other members of the school community followed. I was instrumental in devising work schemes, initiating discussion about the school brochure, policy statements, involving outside agencies in school and so on. However, I felt that I was, at the same time, responsible for making the vision-building process a collective one. The image of our school in the future was emerging as we progressed. It was an evolutionary process and it is still taking place as the school moves on and the vision develops.

During this process I tried to balance creativity and organisational trust. A firm foundation based on the value systems laid
down by me had been highlighted by decisions which I made,
particularly during the early months of my headship. My impression
when I visited the school (which was upheld when I took up the
post) was that very little was valued. The children, staff, internal
environment, materials, resources etc. were in need of stimulation.
The human resources were undervalued, underused, demotivated
and demoralised. The children's work was poorly displayed, sparse,
kept in old cardboard boxes and lay in discarded piles. The resources
were antiquated, in a poor state of repair, inaccessible to the
children, drab and unattractive. Quality was the key to moving
towards a more effective school but it was, at that time, missing.
Quality in terms of resources was totally lacking and the qualities
residing in the staff were dormant. I needed to create a quality
environment within the school. Initially it was simply necessary to
remove all the rubbish, to talk to children, staff and governors and
to organise the school to establish a base on which to build. As part
of the ongoing process I had, as a starting point, to communicate
my vision and to secure commitment among other members of the
organisation. This required communication of meaning.

In the search for quality I began by raising the standard of
displays within the school. I only accepted the best that the children
could attain and I insisted that work was mounted properly,
displayed effectively and valued accordingly. It had a dramatic
effect, the environment was transformed; the children worked hard
to achieve their best; and the staff were proud of the school and
eager to share it with visitors. This reinforced the view of, among
others, Beare, Caldwell and Millikan, that a shared vision must be
articulated by the leader and pervade day-to-day activities:

> the leader articulates the vision in such compelling ways that
> it becomes the shared vision of the leader's colleagues and it
> illuminates their ordinary activities with dramatic significance
> (Beare, Caldwell and Millikan 1989, p.109).

The staff, particularly in a small primary school, must see that
the headteacher is an effective practitioner. It is not enough to have
a vision, it must be operationalised and thus they lead by example.
Coulson (1986, p.85) considers that:

> Successful heads have a vision of how they would like to
> see their schools and thus they give their schools a sense
> of direction but importantly they also are capable of
> operationalising their goals and values both through a long
> term strategy and at the level of day-to-day actions.

Peters and Waterman (1982), in their discussion of a value-shaping leader, mention that he/she must instil enthusiasm through scores of daily events and become an implementer par excellence. I consider that as a leader I must exhibit teaching expertise and my commitment to the value systems which will produce a quality education for the children.

Parental involvement and communication with the village community was essential in establishing value systems which would encourage commitment to quality. I made it clear that I needed their help to improve aspects of school life. Tangible evidence of improvement came in many guises.

The breadth of literature available to the children was restricted. During the first term I was at the school we organised a book fair and bought books with the commission which we earned. I applied for a grant for books from the Senior Inspector for English to supplement what was in the library and we introduced a new reading scheme which would be complemented by the books already present. Variety, availability and enthusiasm for books were key elements which were needed to achieve excellence. The nuclear school community, i.e. caretaker, secretary, teacher, cook helped to remove everything which was clearly past its 'sell by date'. Parents and governors put up shelves, removed and reorganised furniture and carried out other similar tasks. The base line was created and my intention to strive for excellence was founded, a perspective shared by West-Burnham (1992, p.117):

> In the context of total quality management, the primary
> responsibility of leadership is to create the environment in
> which continuous improvement can take place.

I felt that this was, and still is, one of my main aims to enable a school to keep moving forward on the path to improvement.

Another key element in establishing a quality education within the school was staff development. As an integral part of the growth of the school, the needs and professional development of the teaching staff had to be facilitated. In the first instance it was appropriate to concentrate on improving classroom performance and thus providing a better learning environment. To facilitate this I invited several advisory teachers to work in school alongside staff to provide subject expertise and to act as staff development agents. The decision to initiate our staff development programme in school was successful because it went a long way to meeting the immediate perceived needs of the staff and the school.

Alongside this approach in the school, I was aware that other schools in the proposed cluster were developing in a similar way. In a rural environment where all the schools are very small, networking seemed to be a necessary next step. A meeting was organised to discuss common staff development issues and a nominated representative from each school, in some cases the headteacher, attended. I was invited to lead the group by my colleagues because I had several years' experience in this field. Our cluster consists of seven small rural primary schools and one secondary school. Initially staff development activities were planned to meet identified group needs. My role as leader of this group of schools needed the same skills as my role as headteacher in my own institution. My capacity to lead and ability to manage would be illustrated by my skill as a planner, organiser, trainer, communicator, co-ordinator, innovator, representative, administrator, problem-solver, decision-maker, evaluator and chairman.

My vision of the future of support through networking began with its base in a professional development programme. The next step, which was part of the evolutionary process towards the vision, was to set up a forum for headteachers to meet and discuss key issues, to make joint decisions on common topics and to invite informed outside agencies to contribute to the work of our cluster. One visible outcome of the work of this group was a booklet produced by the headteachers as a marketing tool. *Village Schools Facing the Challenge* was an attempt to answer many questions which had arisen from informal discussions, open evenings, local press coverage, and so on, about the ability of small schools to deliver the National Curriculum. As time has passed, this group has become indispensable to all its members. Our strength is as a group and in the support which we offer to each other. Our vision for the continuation of the cluster is inevitably intertwined with the future of the individual schools within it. We have similar value bases as we all serve rural communities and feel that we have a great deal to offer.

I have discussed several definitions of vision, my interpretation of them, my application of my vision within the school and the cluster in which I lead the team. The school has developed considerably from the position at which I became headteacher. Once a vision for the school was evolving it became necessary to state a clear idea of purpose which could be incorporated in a mission statement but it is always important to remember that:

> a key ingredient in the notion of mission is that it should
> excite, stimulate and motivate all members of the school
> (Holly and Southworth 1989, p.51).

This shows the link between vision and mission. The mission statement must include the values and purpose which will motivate the staff to move forward. Expressing this in written form is a strategic activity at the level of whole school planning which is a task for governors and the headteacher in consultation with other members of the school community. The mission statement needs to fulfil the need to articulate vision within individual institutions. It should be a useful tool and provides a series of functions:

- it characterises the school to its community
- it provides a sense of direction and purpose
- it serves as a criterion for policy making
- it sets the school culture
- it generates consistency of action
- it identifies clients
- it serves to motivate and challenge.

(West Burnham 1992, p.71).

This definition is thorough and detailed and sets out the need to clarify vision into practical purpose. After discussion with governors and staff we adopted the mission statement for our school which is shown in the box below:

Mission Statement

The school will provide a stimulating environment to enable all pupils to attain high levels of achievement, whilst catering for individual needs — providing appropriate resources, managed through open and effective communication.

I was aware that the statement needed to be concise but also that it must inform management decisions. The key element of education within a small primary school is the possibility of meeting individual needs. This is central to all planning, provision and decision-making. The environment, high levels of attainment and relevant resources are central to the delivery of education within the school. The final component of the statement is instrumental in achieving the rest. However it may need clarification when the statement is reviewed as part of the audit of the School Development Plan.

The mission statement is broken down into the school's aims. The school identified key areas which are represented below:

- to help pupils to develop lively, inquiring minds, to acquire knowledge and develop skills of communication and infor-mation which will equip them for adult life;
- to receive challenging and enjoyable experiences in the belief that living fully in each stage of development is important;

- to help pupils to appreciate and be concerned about their environment and to understand the interdependence of individuals, groups and nations in our world;
- to help pupils to achieve self discipline and commitment so that they reach the highest standards of which they are capable;
- to encourage pupils to develop creativity and expression in the arts and physical activity;
- to encourage regular communication and dialogue with parents;
- to ensure a safe and well ordered school environment.

The continuing cycle of planning enables us to keep moving towards an ever-changing vision whilst striving to achieve the aims of the school. There are key elements which are central to the future development of the school. These are quality provision of an educational experience, the achievement of individual excellence to match ability, support for staff development and the taking on board of the changes in the broader educational environment.

In moving forward, the cluster schools must strengthen their group identity in order not only to survive but to provide the best possible service for the pupils. The cluster has organised a series of joint activity days for peer groups of children. These involve all the children from one year group, for example, Year 6, meeting together at one venue to focus on a curriculum area. There have been maths, English and music days to date. This is one way to meet the demands of specialist teaching for upper primary children, providing a peer group experience and at the same time, delivering effective staff development. These sessions are all led by curriculum specialists.

It is always necessary to look to the future in terms of staff provision so I have set up a support group for supply staff in the area. Many of the permanent appointments which will be made in the next few years will come from the supply staff that we use on a regular basis. I see it as essential that they are trained, updated, informed and valued.

The financial aspect of the future for small schools is the most threatening. Now that the transitional support has ended and the formula structure has been altered, rural schools are faced with the prospect of diminishing financial resources. It seems inevitable that very small primary schools like this one will close because they are not economically viable. However, the result of allowing this to happen is the slow decline of the villages and the dales which they serve. The population base may slowly move to the site of the central school which would further the depopulation of rural areas.

An alternative to financing schools as individual institutions would be to fund the cluster schools as one (see Figure 3.1). There

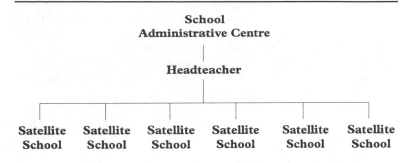

Figure 3.1 Cluster schools

would be one main school and administrative centre where the governing body and the headteacher of all the schools could be based. A senior teacher could be based in each individual institution with responsibility for the daily operation of the school. The schools would have one vision, mission statement and set of aims and objectives.

The main school could be responsible for hosting joint activity days for the peer group specialist input, it could act as the training centre for staff etc. while allowing each institution to function as part of the whole but with an independent building situated in the local community. Of course the problems with this scenario arise because each school has a separate Governing Body under present legislation. Planning at national and LEA level is short-sighted in that the solution to the problem seems to be to close small schools on financial grounds and then to deal with the consequences as they arise. In our area this would mean a considerable building programme on at least one site because none of the schools within a ten mile radius could accommodate any more children. There is no meaningful discussion taking place to form a cohesive, coherent response to the challenge of the future. Informal meetings between headteacher colleagues are the only forum at local level where concerns are vocalised. The LEA is 'clutching at straws' to save the services it can continue to provide and does not offer a lead to schools on the problems.

Another option would be for a school or a cluster of schools to apply for grant-maintained status. At the present time the governing body of the school is opposed to this on political grounds. It is not under consideration at all. They see it as the quickest route to closure and prefer the 'wait and see' approach. Many small primary schools are investigating the potential benefits of this option which, they believe, could mean survival.

The choice to keep individual schools in local communities open with one central governing body, headteacher and administrative centre would be the best option in my view. There would be organisational problems and it is probably already too late to be a realistic choice. However, the benefits would give flexibility and life to the rural communities which are in danger of becoming more isolated.

Conclusion

There is a broad consensus amongst authors about the issues surrounding vision and mission and the leadership role needed to deliver them effectively. The description offered by Peters (1988, p.14) rings very true with schools. He says that the vision:

> must act as a compass in a wild stormy sea — but like a compass must be adjusted continually to take account of its surroundings.

A clear and powerful vision will set out the unique purpose of a particular school or group of schools and will give a sense of 'belonging' to the community of the school. The whole group must be committed if a vision is to be realised. It will transform the ordinary life of the school into something challenging. Fullan (1992) discusses developing collaborative cultures, vision as 'emergent and flexible' and the leader's role as learning as well as leading. These factors are central to my experience as a manager both in my own institutions and in the cluster of primary schools.

References

Beare, H., Caldwell, B.J. and Millikan, R.H. (1989) *Creating an Excellent School* Routledge.

Bennis, W. and Nanus, B. (1985) *Leaders* Harper and Row: New York.

Coulson, A. (1986) *The Managerial Work of Primary School Headteachers* Sheffield Papers in Education Management No 48, Sheffield Hallam University.

Davies, B. and Ellison, L. (1992) *School Development Planning* Longman.

Day, C., Whitaker, P. and Johnson, D. (1990) *Managing Primary Schools in the 1990s* Paul Chapman Publishing Ltd.

Fullan, M.G. (1992) *Successful School Improvement* Open University Press.

Holly, P. and Southworth, G. (1989) *The Developing School* Falmer Press.

Peters, T. (1988) *Thriving on Chaos* Macmillan.

Peters, T. and Waterman, R.H. (1982) *In Search of Excellence* Harper Collins.

West-Burnham, J. (1990) 'Human resource management in schools' in Davies, B., Ellison, L., Osborne, A. and West-Burnham, J. *Education Management for the 1990s* Longman.

West-Burnham, J. (1992) *Managing Quality in Schools*, Longman.

4 Managing the post National Curriculum

Rosemary Thorn and Allan Osborne

In the midst of an unprecedented structural and legal reform of education, it is sometimes necessary to remind ourselves of 'the basics' – that a school should always be a place of learning. A 'good school' will be one which concentrates its major energies on teaching and learning. It is a school where teaching and learning is the prime purpose of everyone connected with the school and to which all aspects of management must be constantly directed. The only schools to achieve lasting success will be 'learning schools' where teachers, adults and children alike learn. In these schools new ideas and innovations will be viewed as positive educational challenges, rather than as structural or bureaucratic shifts, and all concerned will work closely together to integrate the new with the old in the best interests of the children and their learning.

It is a reasonably common, although not uncontentious, view that the curriculum is the total learning experience which every child receives and enjoys. This view encompasses both the formal subjects of the National Curriculum and the many facets of the hidden curriculum. These facets are to be seen in the ethos of the school, in the way it celebrates success and supports difficulties and disappointments, in the way children and adults behave individually and interact with one another and in the way in which they respond to their world. In short, the curriculum is the very essence of the

learning school: it is both its life blood and its life-giving force —
indeed its very *raison d'etre*.

Whilst much of what follows apparently concerns itself with
the narrower (or overt) curriculum, there can be little doubt that
the manner in which curriculum planning and implementation are
carried out will have profound implications upon the nature of the
broad educational experience of everyone associated with the school.
Since every child has a right to the best possible education, then it is
incumbent upon the headteacher and everyone else connected with
the school, to ensure that each and every child receives this. The
idea of the curriculum is both the conceptual and practical means
to this end; and as such must be managed in such a way to ensure
that it provides:

- the opportunity to achieve high academic standards;
- complete coverage of all the required statutory elements and
  other desirable elements;
- continuity and progression for every child with just enough
  repetition to allow for consolidation and higher level con-
  ceptualisation;
- the freedom to develop at an individual pace;
- the flexibility to cater for particular talents and/or difficulties.

In short, the curriculum must ensure the most appropriate
learning experiences for every child throughout his/her time in
school.

Before 1989 primary schools had almost complete freedom
with regard to curriculum matters; but the phased introduction
of the National Curriculum has ended this freedom by establishing
programmes of study (POS) for each subject and key stage, attainment targets (ATs) and statements of attainment (SOA) with which
all schools must comply. Between 1989 and 1992 these were introduced for the core subjects of English, mathematics and science
and the foundation subjects of technology, history, geography, art,
music and physical education. Each local education authority (LEA)
or board of education for church aided schools also produced its
own document for the basic curriculum of religious education. All
schools must comply with these legal requirements and with the
related aspects of the assessment of children's learning and reporting
to parents.

Chapter 3 discussed the importance of having a vision for the
school and of involving all the stakeholders in its development. Just
as the curriculum is the central purpose of a school, so the shared
curriculum-focused vision should be the core of the whole school
vision. Indeed it is probable that the only effective whole school

vision is the one which is conceptualised and realised through the curriculum.

In terms of managing the curriculum there are basically three interlinking and interdependent levels each with its own timescale. These are:

1. The long-term level — which relates to the whole school, is identified in the school development plan and has a time span of up to five years.
2. The medium-term level — which begins to translate the whole school plans into action. These plans are concerned with the curriculum for a particular subject, a key stage and/or year group, they highlight aspects of the development plan and usually have a time-scale of one to three years.
3. The short-term level — which is the stage at which detailed arrangements are made to ensure the effective learning of particular groups of children. The cycles for this vary as they are dependent upon the particular circumstances. Planning at this level incorporates arrangements for particular topics, themes or subjects and programmes for individual children.

These management levels for curriculum matters link closely and respectively with the strategic, tactical and operational levels identified by Ellison and Davies (1990) and applied to all aspects of school management. This requires linking in more detail with curriculum management and the roles of individuals.

The National Curriculum is the legal framework within which all maintained schools must operate. The headteacher is directly responsible for the curriculum which the school provides and for ensuring that it is compatible with all legal requirements. He/she is accountable for this ultimately to the Department for Education (DfE) but, more directly and immediately, to the consumers (the children and their parents), the school's governing body and, where appropriate, to the LEA. There are also close links between the curriculum and other sections of the 1988 Education Reform Act. For example the resourcing of the curriculum depends upon formula funding which in turn depends upon the number of pupils which is determined by open enrolment and parental choice. Thus the management of the curriculum is crucial for the continuing success of the school.

Responsibility and accountability for the curriculum rests with the headteacher but it is also true that the volume and range of responsibilities and tasks required by recent legislation has made it essential to use delegation and empowerment as management strategies in curriculum matters if the headteacher is not to be totally overwhelmed. These strategies also fit well with the principles of

sharing and ownership. It is vitally important for the organisational
health of the school and for its curriculum that there is open
discussion on curriculum matters and that the decision-making
process is clear and truly participative. This ensures a genuine
feeling of sharing and ownership and therefore guarantees implementation — often the neglected child of planning.

However it is important to remember that the headteacher is just
that, the school's leading practitioner and that he/she was appointed
at least as much for curriculum expertise as for management skill.
The introduction of local management of schools (LMS) and grant-
maintained status (GMS) has not changed the fact that overall
curriculum management remains his/her prime responsibility. An
adjunct to this is that many headteachers have not experienced the
National Curriculum as class teachers and some even feel that they
have been deskilled by recent events and have lost some expertise
and credibility. Where this applies it is essential that the headteacher
considers his/her own professional development and arranges the
daily management of the school to enable him/her to have a more
direct involvement in curriculum matters.

Whilst retaining overall curriculum leadership and responsibility for management, it is important that the headteacher utilises
fully the experience and expertise of key members of staff, e.g. the
deputy headteacher, the post-holders and curriculum and subject
co-ordinators. An on-going staff development programme should
enable them to take a full part in the management of the curriculum
and to accept meaningful responsibility for clearly defined elements.
Where a school has a shared and curriculum-centred vision, delegation
and empowerment will be both more realistic and more effective.

Against such a background, it is now appropriate to consider
some practical aspects of curriculum management. Children are at
the heart of the educational process and it is essential to retain this
priority at all times. So, whilst the curriculum can conceptually have
an existence of its own, it can only achieve its full value, and thus
be fully justified, when it is closely correlated with the requirements
of teaching and learning in relation to the needs of the children.
The curriculum should exist to facilitate the teaching and learning
process; it must be a valuable tool which helps the teaching staff to
provide a beneficial, effective and appropriate learning experience
for every child.

It may be argued that the advent of the National Curriculum
has taken freedom of choice from schools and has obviated the
need for curriculum planning. But this view is based upon a
misunderstanding of the relationship between planning and implementation. In fact, effective planning which considers implementation
issues is now more necessary than ever. For example, schools must

make decisions about whether the National Curriculum will be taught through cross-curricular topics or through specific subjects. As with so many issues it is finding the correct balance which is the key to success. Some subjects, especially English and mathematics, will probably continue to be taught as individual subjects whereas overlapping programmes of study, e.g. in geography and science, suggest that a cross-curricular topic would be more appropriate. It is essential that very careful thought is given to this to ensure that all subject-specific skills are included and that, to prevent curriculum overload, no unplanned overlap or repetition occurs. In the primary school this is particularly important at Key Stage 2 where the programmes of study contain a great deal of material. To ensure effective teaching and learning it is also important to consider ways of introducing some specialist teaching to ensure that pupils have stimulating materials and presentation and that there is a reasonable balance of subjects.

The only sure way to achieve this curriculum cohesion over time is by using a comprehensive planning process which will enable every child to receive, throughout their years in the primary school, a broad and balanced curriculum which provides for continuity, progression and differentiation without undue repetition.

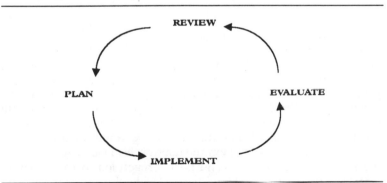

Figure 4.1 The planning cycle

Planning is a cyclical process which is often shown as in Figure 4.1. However, as the needs of the child are central to the planning process and must be considered at all times, it may be more suitable to consider the planning process as a wheel with the child as the hub. (See Figure 4.2) The spokes of the wheel highlight both the relationship between the child and the planning process and the interdependence of the two.

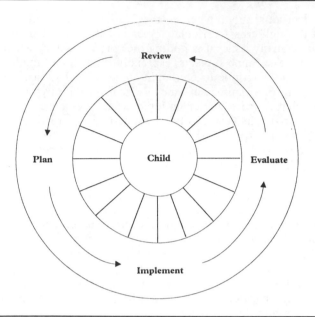

Figure 4.2   The relationship between the child and the planning process

An effective curriculum relies on the support of clear management processes which enable every facet of a child's educational needs to be met and this can perhaps best be achieved through a series of interlocking and interdependent curriculum plans. These plans can be fitted into the model for strategic, tactical and operational levels with the child as the pinnacle and the school as the base, although timescales will be both variable and overlapping — the 'model' must not dictate the process (see Figure 4.3).

Each of these plans follows the same cycle of elements. However the length of these cycles, the number of repetitions per year and the formality of the process should vary considerably. For example the whole school plan has one cycle per year, it functions through formal meetings and it is fully documented — although it should be set in the context of a longer-term (three to five years) directional plan. At the other extreme, topic plans have one cycle per topic with six to ten topics per class per year, rely more heavily on informal meetings and professional dialogue and emphasise practical rather than formal documentation.

It is becoming evident that the number and variety of the types of curriculum plans mean that while the ideal, in terms of vision, ownership and participative management, would be for

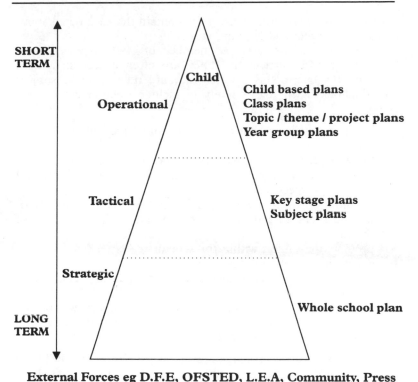

SHORT TERM

Child

Operational

Child based plans
Class plans
Topic / theme / project plans
Year group plans

Tactical

Key stage plans
Subject plans

Strategic

Whole school plan

LONG TERM

External Forces eg D.F.E, OFSTED, L.E.A, Community, Press

Figure 4.3   Planning levels

everyone to be involved in all the planning levels, the reality is that constraints of time, human and physical resources mean that this is unrealistic. However, it is important that the decision-making process, as distinct from the decision-taking process, is structured to enable everyone to be fully involved in the consultation process.

The size and nature of the school, its management style and structure and the roles and job descriptions of individuals all influence the curriculum management process. In most schools the class teacher is responsible for the day-to-day management of the curriculum for his/her class and is directly responsible for this, depending on the size and organisation of the school, to the year group leader, key stage leader, deputy headteacher or headteacher. Where the size of the school permits, the class teachers co-operate closely with colleagues in the same year groups to plan the topics which form the major part of the curriculum. These are the operational or short term plans. They contain the most detail about objectives, content and teaching strategies.

Most schools also have a member of staff responsible for each area of the curriculum. They are often called curriculum co-ordinators but in this chapter they are referred to as subject co-ordinators. Their role is likely to include some or all of these facets:

• be interested in, enthusiastic about and have expertise in the subject;
• know the legal requirements/recommendations for the subject;
• be clear about its place within the school and the local and national perspectives;
• be familiar with resources available and desirable;
• be well prepared and able to explain and justify all aspects of the subject;
• promote the subject within the school;
• act as an exemplar to colleagues;
• encourage others, listen to concerns and provide action plans for them;
• assume responsibility for managing the subject within the school, e.g. documentation, planning, implementation, assessment, record-keeping and evaluation.

In terms of curriculum planning, their main input will be at the tactical or medium-term level where it is their management role to see that the requirements of their subjects are being met. However, it is important to see these people in close liaison with both class teachers at the operational stage and with curriculum co-ordinators and senior staff at the strategic planning stage.

A very important role within the school is that of a curriculum co-ordinator such as the head of infants or a Key Stage co-ordinator. These people have a very different role from that of the subject co-ordinator as their management responsibility in curriculum terms is for the total curriculum and pastoral care for all the children within that part of the school. Their major input too is at the tactical or medium-term level, e.g. the key stage plans. However their influence also goes well beyond this — as their role means that they will need to be involved at both the strategic and operational levels. Appropriate processes and mechanisms will be required to achieve these different areas of interaction — they will not just happen!

The long-term or strategic level may be seen to receive its main input from the headteacher, deputy headteacher and the curriculum sub-committee of the governing body. This is the level which formally verbalises the school's curriculum vision,

forms the basis of the management plan, ensures compatibility
with all the legal requirements, links with the development plan
and INSET programme and indicates the level of funding needed.
This plan is the least practically-based of all the plans but its aims
and philosophy must be incorporated and visible within all the other
plans. In fact, all the different levels of curriculum planning must
be totally consistent with each other.

The importance of this comprehensive approach to planning
cannot be over-estimated. Such a process can only be achieved if all
those affected feel that they have been able to contribute. Clearly, it
is not possible or practical for everyone to attend every meeting but
it should be possible to secure a participative process involving full
consultation — a particular task of the headteacher. The success of
the school's curriculum, and hence of the school itself, is dependent
upon this plan and therefore it is of paramount importance that the
process, as well as the content, is right for the school.

Given that the aim of the curriculum is to provide a quality
educational experience for every child, then the planning must

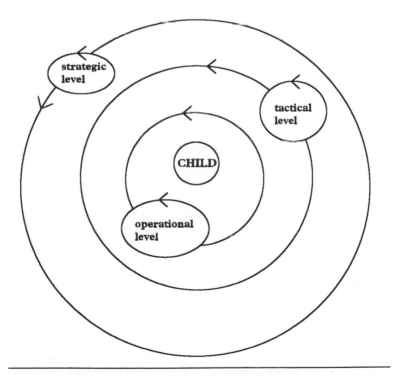

Figure 4.4   The child's perspective on plans

always put the child's needs first. From the child's perspective, the range of plans may be expressed as a solar system model with each type of plan turning at its own rate and completing an appropriate number of cycles each year as in Figure 4.4. In this model the strongest force is the one which focuses inwards onto the child.

From the headteacher's perspective the model may appear to be reversed i.e. with the strategic plan at the centre as this is the main thrust of the headteacher's personal input (see Figure 4.5). In this model the strongest force is the outward one by which the curriculum provided influences every aspect of a child's development.

The reality is that both of these perspectives are equally important for the education and well-being of the child and for the organisational health of the school. Each plan is interlinked with the other so that there is full compatibility between them. In each case the shorter-term one contains the essence of the longer-term one and the longer-term one forms part of the continuous chain between the child and the legal framework.

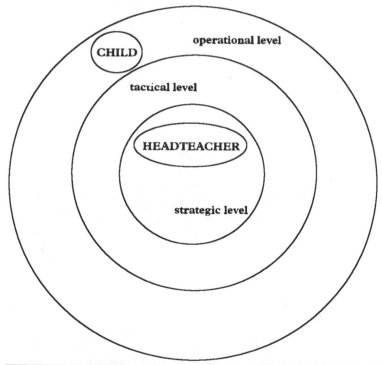

Figure 4.5   The headteacher's perspective on plans

Every school has to have a range of curriculum documentation to fulfil its statutory requirements and to prepare itself for the OFSTED inspection arrangements. It is important for each school to consider its own needs in relation to these requirements and then to set out a detailed plan itemising the action needed and the appropriate timescale. This management perspective could be outlined in the development plan and, in more detail, in the whole school curriculum plan.

Whilst reiterating that the overall aim of the curriculum is to provide the best possible education for each and every child, it is appropriate to consider in more detail the purpose of the different plans and finally to consider the staffing implications of such a planning process.

Long-term/strategic plan

This sets out the curriculum vision of the school and expresses the principles and aims on which the whole curriculum is based. It provides a framework for the other plans needed. It is a map which shows how the school's curriculum fits with national and local requirements and guidelines, discusses teaching styles and strategies, details the timescale for curriculum development work, outlines the INSET programme to support it, gives information about the human and physical resources available, and states the arrangements for teacher and statutory assessment.

This plan is very important from both management and practical perspectives. It is the plan with which all the others must comply and therefore it is important that everyone should feel involved in it as it must be shared and owned. The management responsibility for this rests with the headteacher and the main input in this is from the headteacher, deputy headteacher, curriculum sub-committee of the governing body and the curriculum co-ordinators within the school. However, if it is to influence classroom practice, everyone must participate and feel that they have had every opportunity to express their views.

Medium-term/tactical plans

The key stage plans begin the process of working out, from a practical perspective, exactly how the National Curriculum will operate within the school. Through these plans continuity and progression are assured, needless repetition is avoided and a broad, balanced and relevant educational experience is achieved over time. They ensure that the programme of study for each subject is covered, that an appropriate subject balance is achieved for each year group and that all required assessments are made.

The management responsibility for these key stage plans rests with the curriculum or key stage co-ordinators. There will, however, also be considerable input from the headteacher and deputy head-teacher to ensure compatibility with the whole school plan, from the subject co-ordinators (as desired) and from the class teachers. This involvement ensures ownership and, thus, commitment to the implementation of the plans.

Similarly, whilst the individual subject co-ordinators would be empowered to manage the development of the subject plans, the management responsibility for ensuring their compatibility with the overall plan is shared between them and the headteacher and deputy headteacher. The subject plans show how the school's curriculum approach fits with and responds to the requirements, recommendations and guidance of both national and local govern-ment initiatives.

Every teacher will be expected to implement these plans and so it is of vital importance that, as far as practicable, everyone is involved in drawing them up. Certainly everyone must be actively involved in the full consultation process.

Short-term/operational plans

These are the detailed plans which consider the topics, themes and subjects for each group of children and which provide the outline ideas and then the precise activities needed fully to implement the medium- and long-term plans. These are the plans which are closest to the child and, as such, the management responsibility for them rests with those who deliver the curriculum, i.e. the class teachers. They may either work on these along with, or in close co-operation with, a colleague. Collaborative planning at this level usually happens most easily in the larger primary schools where there are two or more parallel classes. However, it is so valuable in terms of human and physical resources, especially time, that it would be beneficial and profitable for smaller schools to find ways of introducing this.

The necessary integration of both the planning process and the plans which arise from it suggests that a large number of people is needed to achieve success. Ten subject co-ordinators, two curriculum co-ordinators (one for each key stage), deputy headteacher, headteacher, governors and, of course, the class teach·

ers will all be involved. If this were the case, then clearly no primary school would be able to manage its curriculum in this way. However, primary school teachers have always been accustomed to undertaking a wide range of tasks, duties and responsibilities, although this has never been more so than in the 1990s. The vast majority of teachers now fulfil either a multi-faceted role or have several specific roles. Even in a large school, a curriculum co-ordinator is also likely to be a subject co-ordinator and a class teacher. All class teachers, except those in their first year of teaching, will almost certainly be subject co-ordinators as well. In a small school the number and diversity of roles is likely to be even greater, e.g. the deputy headteacher may also be a curriculum co-ordinator, a subject co-ordinator and a class teacher.

This multiplicity of roles means that the same person will often be involved from slightly different standpoints in long-term, medium-term and short-term planning, but always with the aim of providing the best education for the children. Paradoxically then, it may be this multi-role situation which helps to ensure successful curriculum management as it guarantees involvement, co-operative ways of working and participative management styles and processes. The key to the success is an owned and shared curriculum vision to which everyone is totally committed. However, this vision will never become a reality without appropriate leadership at all levels. It is suggested here that the best way to achieve this is through a structured professional development programme. This will involve, over time, a series of whole school, group and individual activities which would enable each member of staff to develop the knowledge and skills needed for successful curriculum leadership and management and to receive appropriate support when tackling new tasks. This programme will also show all staff that their own contributions are truly valued and with this sense of value will come increased motivation and a positive response to empowerment and delegated responsibility as each seeks to realise his/her own potential.

The emphasis of this chapter has been on the centrality of the curriculum to the purpose of the school, on the extreme importance of curriculum planning and on the professional development needed to achieve it. However, it must also be said that all aspects of the curriculum planning cycle are important. Whenever development work is to be done the present situation must be reviewed and used as the starting point and to inform practice. Equally, the implementation of the plans must be carefully monitored to ensure that they are being enacted. Even more important is evaluation, both the formal evaluation of each activity and the informal on-going evaluation. Informal evaluation may be a chat over a cup of coffee or a longer discussion after school. This latter is, perhaps, the most significant approach in that it frequently has an immediate effect on practice. Such evaluation also provides an immediate link with the quality dimension as it is concerned with ensuring that the curriculum provided is both effective and efficient, but elements of formal evaluation will already have been built into the different plans — won't they?

Reference

Ellison, L. and Davies, B. (1990) 'Planning in education management' in Davies, B., Ellison, L., Osborne, A. and West-Burnham, J. *Education Management for the 1990s* Longman

5 Managing staff — I have seen the future and it works . . . possibly

Malcolm Lister

Introduction

In this chapter I wish to advocate a policy of proactivism and self-determination as the most logical and comfortable means by which schools can face the future with confidence and optimism. I intend to focus upon the staff of the school and to indicate some aspects of personnel management, support and development that should (with luck) assist both institutional and individual needs. It is hardly coincidental that the OFSTED *Framework for Inspection* (OFSTED 1993) indicates the importance of a school's ethos and sense of purpose, as well as the quality of leadership, school self-evaluation and development planning. These are among the issues to be explored in the ensuing sections.

Oppressive gloom should not necessarily be the prevailing orthodoxy. Staffroom conversation is not always dominated by discussion about the merits of valium or yearnings for early retirement. Despite contradictory evidence that schools have simply been given too much to do and that the system is sagging under the weight of information and expectation, the service has not crumbled. Schools have battled through. Glimmers of hope, such as the Dearing reforms, are clearly evident.

The school vernacular is currently littered with choice phrases such as 'innovation fatigue', 'relentless change' and 'curriculum overload'. This potentially doom-laden terminology is depressingly familiar and is perhaps symptomatic of the way in which some schools choose to interpret their present predicament. The language we use positively exudes a preoccupation with pressure, stress and diminished morale and motivation. By suggesting that schools are performing well despite the pressures which they face I lay myself open to accusations of unsubstantiated optimism and crass generalisation. There is no intention to wallpaper over the cracks by misguidedly proposing that things are not as bad as they might seem. Yet we surely need to be more positive about our predicament if we are to survive future traumas and turmoil. We might begin by being totally realistic and pragmatic about our current situation. Only then can we face the future confidently and positively by determinedly planning for it. We need to have in place a variety of strategies that will provide us with the means to cope with the pressures and assuredly exploit the opportunities that will undoubtedly arise.

Schools will achieve their aims more readily if they focus upon the individuals who work within the institution and ensure that they really do invest in people. The proposition that 'the staff of a school is its most valuable resource' is by now an exhausted platitude. It is, however, a statement that cannot and should not be ignored. Schools must undertake some form of personnel audit according to procedures and priorities which they themselves establish and within a framework that accurately reflects the current and potential future working environment. They will need to compile a 'human jigsaw' of performance, practice, professionalism, potential and policy which adequately sets the school and its personnel in context and co-existence. As well as providing a fundamental policy statement for the school, such a device can then offer a blanket of comfort and security for individual staff, particularly if they are given the opportunity to participate in its formulation.

The starting point will depend upon the school. In recent years it has been easy to identify among teaching colleagues a pervasive sense of bewilderment and frustration at a system which, in their view, failed to recognise their skills, reward their efforts or offer any logically progressive career structure. There was almost an identity crisis for certain individuals who felt that their roles and responsibilities had been redefined for them without their collusion. The key issues of declining morale and motivation were immediately highlighted when speculation about the future was enduringly bleak. It is pitifully obvious that, if such circumstances exist, there will be a corresponding need to provide some glimmer of light at the end of a particularly dark tunnel. That light has to be identified and progress has to be made inexorably toward it. In our school,

for example, we chose to focus on staff welfare and development.
We set this within the context of current circumstances facing the
school whilst paying particular attention to the potential twin perils
of morale and motivation as mentioned above. We worked with
the presupposition that any member of staff who felt unwilling to
invest effort into identifying matters of personal concern so that
measures could be taken to improve them was probably beyond
the capacity for redemption in the first place! There has to be a tacit
assumption in this process that individuals are actually interested in
their own welfare. Similarly, if there are to be benefits arising from
any situational analysis, then there has to be an acceptance that
some change will be inevitable and as change can be uncomfortable,
there may be an element of 'persuasion' necessary for the process
to work. Finally, if staff welfare is to be treated seriously as
an institutional issue, then the focus must not fall exclusively
upon the teaching staff. All those working in the school must be
considered, though in varying degrees according to their particular
roles and responsibilities One possible way forward might be
to become involved in 'investors in people' (IIP) which allows
organisations (including schools) to demonstrate their commitment
to the development of their employees. IIP is a nationally recognised
quality standard and accreditation can be achieved by working with
the local Training and Enterprise Council.

Having already stressed the grip that emotive language can
have on certain situations, the term 'welfare' immediately becomes
susceptible to misinterpretation and challenge. We chose to place
welfare firmly within the overall framework of 'staff development'
and to define it in terms of identifying and attempting to cater
for individual needs. In advocating this process as an essential
preparation for institutional self-determination and control, there
needs to be an acknowledgement that each school is different. It
always was the case and recent legislation which celebrates market
theory clearly ensures that it always will be. The one element of
certainty that can be invoked is that staff development really will
have a clear focus. It has to be tackled at source. Schools which fail
to recognise this inevitability run the risk of wasting opportunities
and surrendering the initiative with the vain hope that salvation will
miraculously materialise from an external source. On the contrary,
we have to look at ourselves and maximise the potential that is
clearly available to most institutions.

Situational analysis

As a starting point, schools will need to undertake a comprehensive
situational analysis of their present position whilst taking into

account, as far as is possible, the various factors that may (or will) impinge upon the progress of the school. Hopefully, the groundwork for this will already have been undertaken as part of schools' increasingly thorough approaches to development planning. Schools need to learn from the positive elements of the planning process whilst embellishing their analysis with pertinent information. An essential ingredient within this process is to stress the positive factors that exist within the school. If we simply allow depressed and demoralised colleagues to comment upon a predictably jaundiced version of the prevailing circumstances we may unwittingly reinforce the damning stereotypes of overwork, poor resourcing and unachievable expectations. These factors must not be ignored as they obviously exist, yet it is essential that the negatives are counterbalanced by the various positives accessible to the school. This is the beginning of a process of recognising and celebrating a school's strengths and is the essence of acknowledging an individual's worth and contribution. It is the starting point for future staff development.

Our own situational analysis (preparatory questionnaire shown in Figure 5.1) was, predictably, a curate's egg. There was much to feel concerned about but equally plenty for which to be thankful. With staff welfare as our beacon we attempted to rationalise our situation so that we could produce an action plan which took full account of those very factors which could influence the ultimate success or failure of the enterprise. Schools will increasingly require action plans that have realistic, achievable targets but which also take account of the need for flexibility should certain circumstances unexpectedly arise. A fire, a massive staff turnover or an inspection give a small flavour of the type of unplanned-for situation that can, and all too frequently does, occur. Events will be best handled if staff are fully conversant with the plan and what it entails.

It is to be hoped that, over the last few years, the staff of a school will have been regularly consulted during the process of school development planning. Staff development planning should be just part of this overall process but one which really *is* relevant to the staff themselves. To stress an often repeated statement, staff really must have ownership of this particular plan if it is to have any purpose or validity. Also, if it is to be a genuine action plan it must be on-going. Evaluation must be built in and regular re-appraisal of particular elements is an essential feature if adjustments are necessary due to a change in focus or direction.

The focus on staff welfare in our school can best serve as a paradigm for the type of approach to personnel management and development that I wish to advocate. Schools will not necessarily have the same priorities or concerns yet those which ignore the

The school and you

Would you please complete the following questionnaire so that we can gather together ideas and opinions that will help us to prepare a school development plan? Your ideas will be appreciated.

1. What do you think are the main strengths of the school?

2. What do you think is the single most pressing problem which we ought to tackle as soon as possible (always assuming that there is something that we can do about it)?

3. What basic improvements (if any) might we try to make in the following areas?

    (a) Organisational matters

    (b) Timetable/routines

    (c) Premises

    (d) Quality of information/communications

    (e) Links (external agencies)

4. Is there any particular matter/area that you would like to know more about? (e.g. LEA policies, governors' rights and responsibilities, LMS etc).

5. Within the bounds of realism and funding, is there anything that might be done to provide additional support for individuals in the school?

6. Could we rearrange anything that might enhance your personal welfare or well-being — however simple?

Figure 5.1 Situational analysis questionnaire

welfare of their staff do so at their own risk. There is an obvious
tendency for schools to become increasingly insular and self-obsessed,
particularly as the rigours of local management of schools, league
tables, inspections and the like come increasingly into the picture.
Staff will require clarity regarding the future of the school and
the part which they must play in its development over time. The
situational analysis can then help to shape the future as it forms part
of a process of development generated from within.

Those who work in the school deserve access to information
about the factors that influence their working environment. Analysis
and explanation of particular issues are essential if a climate of
openness is to be achieved and rumour and speculation are to be
quelled. This is not necessarily an easy or even a straightforward
task. Colleagues may not fully understand certain factors. They
may not have the time to become fully immersed in elements of a
plan which they perceive to be primarily a managerial responsibility.
They may also be reluctant to face issues that will undoubtedly, at
some stage, influence their personal career or welfare. All of this
is perfectly understandable. What must be prioritised, however, is
an individual's right to an opportunity to consider or contribute
towards any debate about matters directly affecting him or her. If
knowledge really is power, then colleagues must believe that they
can have access to information and that they are entitled to honest
answers to difficult questions. Verbal flannel can be bracketed with
misplaced optimism. It simply will not do. Realism and pragmatism
are the cornerstones of staff development planning and are best
served by an atmosphere of trust and understanding. It would
be especially helpful if schools were confident enough deliberately
to look beyond the institution for validation of their analyses
and intentions. Governors, local authority representatives and the
broader educational community would undoubtedly have a better
understanding of a school's situation if they were provided with
information beyond the obligatory 'Development Plan'. Welfare
issues could be more keenly focused as a consequence, even if
sympathy or solace were the only outcomes to emerge from essentially impotent external auditors who were *invited* to become
involved rather than arriving as a result of 'top-down', monitorial
dictat. My plea here is for honesty and openness.

When we established our welfare plan, we elected to focus
especially on the elements shown in Figure 5.2. It would not seem
unreasonable to suggest that in differing degrees these elements will
have some relevance to most schools. Our situational analysis was
compiled using a variety of questionnaires and interviews.

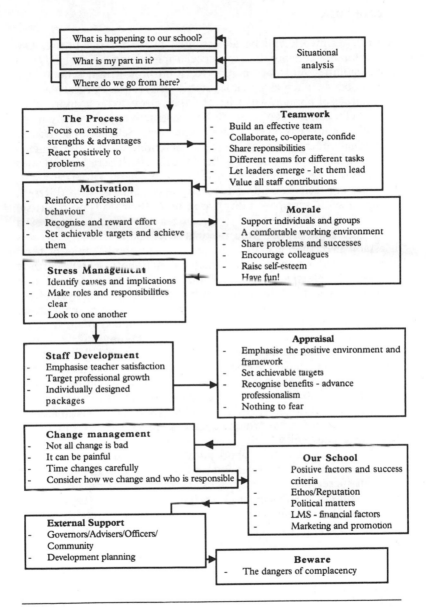

Figure 5.2 A staff development and welfare plan

Teamwork

Clearly, teamwork will be an essential factor for the future. Co-operation and collaboration are crucial ingredients. Workloads and responsibilities must be shared. Relationships within schools will need to be, as much as possible, stable and secure. We must accept that clashes of opinion will arise and that, provided it is approached sensitively, conflict can prove to be constructive, particularly if the prevailing climate is one of support and trust. Schools must harness individual contributions and exploit potential so that the benefits of the team as a whole can be maximised. There are obvious implications for leadership at different levels here. Different teams for different tasks should, it is to be hoped, emerge with different leaders assuming responsibility based upon their skills or expertise. Team decision-making has to become a consistent reality based upon leadership arising from rational discussion. If such a process is established, then it is to be hoped that the commitment of team members will be increased. I believe that most schools already have good, effective teamwork practices to draw upon and that only overtly cynical or deliberately obstructive staff would fail to see the benefits of increased co-operation between colleagues. Current pressures upon schools and the likelihood of little relief in the future suggests that schools must quickly investigate further methods of working together collectively. It would, however, be naive and dangerous to assume that all teams will operate smoothly and consistently. Senior management, as well as delegating a certain level of responsibility to colleagues, must also initiate regular reviews and employ 'servicing' techniques. This might include regular staff development interviews which have clear, pre-set agendas that have been negotiated collectively.

Appropriate INSET opportunities might also arise to support the process. Senior management should be aware that it presides over an increasingly ageing teaching force. 'Servicing' techniques here might entail an element of 'revitalising' the over 40s, through, for example, rotating posts and responsibilities or offering short-term promotions to lead new initiatives. Mentoring and other associated support skills represent other potential areas for consideration.

Finally, there may be a need to deliberately plan team-building exercises and activities to reinforce the advantages of teamwork with colleagues. Any school which pays scant attention to personal and professional relationships runs the risk of inhibiting creative potential, possibly impeded still further by complacency or misplaced optimism.

Motivation

Teamwork will, it is hoped, have a positive spill-over into the area of motivation which is a crucial element in staff welfare. If schools are concerned that motivation is actually threatened by certain factors, then they must identify possible causes and attempt to eradicate them. We chose to echo the work of Maslow (1970) and accept the principle that people work at their best when they are achieving the greatest satisfaction from their work. We need, more then ever, to convince staff that their efforts are recognised, valued and fulfilling. Token 'thank yous' and 'well dones' are insufficient and frequently border on the patronising. I believe that we will constantly need to publicise or even 'market' an individual's contributions. We will need to share successes within the school and publish them as broadly as possible. Governors' reports, the school prospectus, newsletters to parents and the local media are all potential sources. We may feel the need to celebrate an individual's performance more formally through the recognition which a senior colleague can provide during appraisal or performance review sessions.

Schools will need to develop their existing procedures in an effort to obliterate fear or scepticism in favour of enjoyment and a sense of achievement. Job satisfaction is unquestionably at the heart of the motivation process and, in the current climate, a source of potential problems. We must therefore focus more forcefully on those elements of our work which remain worthwhile and challenging to us as professionals. We must emphasise the job enrichment and enjoyment that arises as a result of a task performed successfully. We may have to redefine the way teachers currently view their roles and, in so doing, reemphasise the professionalism and expertise so crudely undermined by recent events. People are more likely to be motivated towards goals that they recognise as important and to which they therefore feel committed. Surely job satisfaction and personal welfare are two such goals? At management level, the real motivation is likely to arise from personal and professional pride in standards achieved and progress made. Neither should loyalty to the school and its aims be overlooked as an additional motivational force.

Morale

Motivation is inextricably linked with morale, another aspect which must be monitored closely. Yet how can schools approach the problem of low morale, especially if the future seems irreversibly bleak? Is morale as low as is claimed and, if so, why? With respect to teachers, our various associations point accusingly at factors such as loss of status, low pay, indiscipline among children, relentless change and a plethora of problems arising from the Government's reforms. Schools will need to identify those elements which directly influence individual and collective morale within the institution. Experience suggests that the sheer unpredictability of a teacher's job lends itself to crisis management and ensuing stress. The current climate whereby schools find themselves uncritically and subserviently enforcing unpalatable legislation or bureaucratic nuances simply exacerbates the situation. Primary teachers in particular have seen their traditional sense of classroom autonomy gradually eroded. At some stage schools will need to come to terms with the new orthodoxy in order that low morale does not become a constant cause of concern. Morale *can* be raised by developing various support strategies and emphasising success and achievement. Some schools may, however, need to sift through the wreckage first of all in order to find those essential glimmers of hope and opportunity. On a more practical note we will also need to accept what our new responsibilities entail, however grudgingly. Only when this is established can we prioritise and select those elements within our role that will engender a much-needed boost to morale. Optimism will not rise if we work in an atmosphere characterised by anxiety, mistrust and frustration. The collective morale of a school is determined by the attitudes and feelings of those who work there. The solution has also to come from within. Early recognition and a determination to arrest the decline are essential prerequisites before any systematic planning can take place to raise morale.

Stress management

Poor morale and motivation invariably lead to stress. If the plethora of protestations about teacher stress emanating from the professional associations and various commissioned studies is to be believed, then schools face an acute problem. The debate about stress has intensified as public understanding about the nature and causes of the condition has gradually increased. Certainly the number of INSET opportunities with the word 'stress' in the title has mushroomed in recent years. As this constant highlighting of a very real problem becomes an ever-present reality, schools can easily be lulled into a sense of panic as they nervously look for tell-tale signs among staff.

Schools will unquestionably need to be aware of stress but must beware of creating a self-induced pressure-cooker-like institution dominated by efforts at amateur psychiatry. A more sensible and sensitive approach is required. Senior management will need to be cognisant of the way that stress may and does affect their own institution so that various methods of remediation can be introduced to tackle the problem. This will require the involvement of all staff, teaching and support, if it is to be truly effective. This proposal may appear to be a self-evident truth for most school policies and yet those of us who work in education appreciate the difficulties and practical pitfalls of whole-school policy-making. Simply gathering the whole staff together can be an exercise of epic proportions! However, effective strategies for stress management demand a whole-school approach, particularly when the possible causes of stress can be so diverse. In times of recession or public uncertainty colleagues will understandingly be concerned about their own future and that of their families. In terms of stress it is the unknown dimension, that which originates outside school, which is potentially the most damaging. Job security, financial uncertainty, the health of a loved one – these are all serious matters which can manifest themselves into stress-based problems for individuals in school. An increase in stress-related illness is one example of the possible consequences.

Stress management should ideally be an implicit part of any staff welfare policy since factors contributing to stress will almost inevitably arise from issues facing the school – morale, motivation, change management and so on. Many of the institutional problems are relatively simple to identify and have been well catalogued in recent research. These include time management, worries about appraisal, a perceived inability to cope with the excessive demands of the National Curriculum and, increasingly, job insecurity. The school will need to provide a safe haven of understanding and support which recognises individual needs and fears and accepts that external factors will influence an individual's behaviour. Time management, in particular, is an essential strategy for school staff and, paradoxically, investing time into techniques to improve our control over events is both wise and likely to pay dividends. There is then an absolute need to devise collective solutions which are practical, sensitive and reliable. Schools must not simply assume that they possess a stable, caring environment where staff are valued and supported. They may have to plan for it. Failure to do so could lead to unfortunate repercussions for individuals and schools alike.

Staff development

The belief that staff welfare is almost synonymous with staff development has constantly been stressed. The future holds many uncertainties for schools during this extended period of radical change. INSET provision is already increasingly diverse as LEAs, the traditional first choice providers, seek to re-establish a role for themselves. Funding for staff development will continue to fluctuate and, although there has been a productive blossoming of school-based curriculum development, individual needs may ultimately be sacrificed on the altar of institutional or, worse still, governmental priorities. At a time when individual development is absolutely crucial in coming to terms with the sheer enormity of the recent reforms, schools face the danger of adopting a 'group, or gang mentality' that focuses disproportionately on the school's needs rather than those of its staff. This is an easy and understandable path to follow and yet it could be a recipe for disappointment. Schools may become blandly uniform rather than paragons of creativity and spontaneity. We must not stultify individual development, but we can no longer rely on ad hoc opportunism to fulfil individual needs. Schools will need to focus closely on each member of staff when preparing staff development policies. They may need to provide individually designed packages in recognition of the fact that people really *are* different. After all, we already do this for pupils.

A policy which actually involves staff in their own development is an essential pre-requisite. This will require self appraisal and careful matching of school and individual needs. Most crucially, we need the determination to provide for those needs. Hollow promises and conditional proposals will not suffice. If we really believe in staff development and appreciate that, if it is successful, the school will be the ultimate beneficiary, then we must invest time, effort and indeed money into the process. This really is an opportunity to be proactive, to focus on enhancing job satisfaction and professional expertise and to truly prioritise from the various alternative demands for our attention. Neither must we ignore the needs of support staff who may also face uncomfortable changes in their role as their work becomes increasingly specialised. The whole staff must be viewed as a resource of rich potential. This is not to ignore the difficulties which such an exercise may present. We will need to sift through the morass to find satisfaction through the fulfilment of professional obligations and responsibilities. Senior management may need to redefine priorities and commitments yet, despite the support it would muster, schools cannot simply focus on uncovering ways in which teachers have less to do. We should rather find ways in which time is more productively spent. Superficially, everything points to a coherent, collaboratively established, co–ordinated development programme. Yet account still needs to be taken of individual aspirations, attitudes and beliefs. Having advocated consideration of individual needs, there must be no avoidance of the possibility that interpretations of need can, and frequently do, differ. This task may be part adjustment, part persuasion, part reconciliation and part hope!

Appraisal

One key ingredient of the staff development programme will now, almost inevitably, be appraisal. Teachers are likely to respond to proposals for development primarily on the basis of their own perceived levels of competence and their personal knowledge base. Two key elements may block this process: a reluctance to change on the part of the individual and a management perspective which suggests that it already knows what others need and therefore manipulates staff accordingly. Embodied here are the classic dilemmas facing schools embarking upon appraisal. If this is approached insensitively, then the predictable consequences of fear, suspicion, threat and resistance become ominous bedfellows. Despite the genuinely supportive efforts of many schools and local authorities, combined with a resigned acceptance of the inevitability of it all, there remains an understandable scepticism about the bureaucratic intentions of those in power. It appears self-evident that there can be no guarantee that appraisal will be entirely successful, but it will surely be more relevant and pertinent if it is firmly placed within the all-embracing context of staff development and welfare. After all, here is the one formal, obligatory process which intentionally focuses exclusively on an individual. Regulations *do* give legal weight to the positive concepts of 'assisting school teachers to realise their potential and carry out their duties more effectively'.

The means whereby an acceptable policy and a positive climate can be established have been well documented, but successful experience elsewhere and attractively presented frameworks are poor substitutes for a school approach which views appraisal as an integral part of existing staff development programmes rather than a bolt on adjunct, an unfortunate but necessary evil. Appraisal will have to become part of a seamless robe of professional development that is an individual's entitlement rather than an unwelcome imposition. This is again not necessarily easy or painless, but if schools decide that they will emphasise the potential benefits of appraisal they are more likely to provide a process that is comfortably productive. If appraisal is subsumed under the banner of staff development, the residual benefits that might be anticipated from the process could be made clearly apparent to those involved. Most schools would look forward to some of the following rewards for their staff:

- the recognition of effective practice;
- the identification of areas of development with accompanying support and advice following in their wake;
- increased job satisfaction;
- greater confidence and a commensurate improvement in morale for individual teachers;
- the identification of individual INSET needs;
- better professional relationships and communication;
- systematic professional development and career planning.

These are not just noble ideals, they are genuine entitlements which staff development policies will need to address if teachers are to be properly prepared for the new pressures and expectations of the late 1990s. Appraisal demands an atmosphere of trust and openness, yet so does staff development generally. A collectively agreed policy for individual and school development is a useful starting point, especially if the need for confidence and a common sense of purpose is venerated and the requirements of time and energy not underestimated.

Change management

The future will inevitably necessitate change in some form. Change management will become an increasingly significant issue as schools face a turbulent and troubled present, linked to a possibly uncertain, financially stringent future. There is extensive evidence to suggest that schools are becoming used to constant change, leading to the slightly perverse proposal that the one element we *can* rely upon is that there will be change! If this remark seems odiously cynical, it has more than a grain of truth in it. Yet any system which accepts change as a norm slips rudderless into a storm of uncertainty and risks perpetuating a sense of hopelessness and demoralisation. Whenever possible, change must be managed. Planning must embrace the possibility or likelihood of alterations in practices or circumstances. Individuals must be informed of, and prepared for, new roles and responsibilities at the earliest possible opportunity.

The prevailing ethos still requires a climate of support and understanding at all levels, otherwise the endless stream of orders and regulations cascading down from our political masters can be quickly misinterpreted by the bemused and weary teachers as devilish impositions by senior management. The temptation to 'shoot the messenger' is understandable and headteachers in particular can quickly become target practice. Senior managers again need to respond positively, providing a regular stream of information and explanation, valuing discussion and encouraging alternative solutions. Managers must regard themselves both as initiators and recipients of change. They must look for favourable conditions for change and, if necessary, be prepared to undertake a damage limitation exercise as early as possible in order to dispel rumour, speculation and controversy. This process will be particularly important for those schools facing radical changes due to various unforeseen factors. Formula funding has, for example, created circumstances whereby larger class sizes and even teacher redundancy have become realities rather than threats. Schools really must anticipate, predict and prepare. Sudden declamations of crisis are hopelessly damaging and singularly unhelpful. The timing of change becomes an increasingly significant and measured strategy in such predicaments.

The literature on 'change management' is awash with analyses of the resisters and barriers to change. Schools will need to identify the various internal obstructions before seeking less painful or difficult solutions to overcome them. The expression 'change agent' is very familiar to schools. If the collective and individual welfare of the institution is considered to be important, then the deployment of change agents, be they human or material, has to be discussed at the earliest possible stage with perhaps a profit–loss analysis taken regarding their use. The 'change agent' approach can be remarkably successful and yet, in personnel terms, the obvious questions will still need to be asked. Who or what? When and why? To what extent and for how long? For everyone or for a select few? An internal or an external agent? Empowered or empowering?

Change can be refreshing and revitalising. It is not necessarily threatening but if it affects people then individual attitudes and beliefs must be accounted for. One target might be to plan for a 'change environment' in which even the unexpected seems to be less portentous. Schools may have to live with the unexpected for many years so that forward planning and disciplined timing will need to become the norm. It is, for example, perhaps advisable to avoid making momentous or critical decisions at the ends of certain terms when staff are frequently tired, at a low ebb and often feel frustrated. The thrust of this approach is to argue for planning over a much longer time-scale so that colleagues understand their present predicament and have some sense of future progress. It is underpinned by the belief that change takes place most effectively when staff feel that they have control over the process.

The school as an organisation

All the factors discussed above impinge upon the school as an organisation. If we are to view staff development and welfare as positively beneficial (and surely we should) then we must seriously assess the organisational health of the institution. We must be constantly aware of the positive factors within the school and ensure that we regularly celebrate them. Our school ethos and reputation will often depend upon them and if *we* fail to publicise and market our successes, who else is going to do it for us? The staff need their achievements to be applauded for reasons of morale, motivation and deserved recognition. It may be management's job to do it for them, perhaps by instituting policies which ensure that the school's successes — or 'selling points', to put it more crudely — are widely appreciated. The school will also need to come to terms with the vast number of influences that bear down upon it, from legislation to local demand. The emphasis has to change from 'coping' to 'creating'. If we have been offered greater freedom to manage our own affairs under the auspices of LMS, then we must fully exploit our opportunities. The ravages of formula funding, the threat of league tables, the demands of often conflicting legislation will continue to take their toll, but if schools capitulate and allow themselves to sink beneath a welter of paper and propaganda they can never shape their own destiny. What price a staff development and welfare plan in such circumstances? We have to respond positively, define our priorities and invest in our future through the constant care and nurturing of our schools. Most schools already recognise this and respond magnificently. They deserve great credit but they may have to get used to providing the accolades themselves!

Leadership

These are perplexing and bewildering times. The responsibility for maintaining a positive ethos within a sound, productive working environment is a great one. It will require increasing skill and expertise as well as patience and sensitivity. Definitions of successful leadership are as controversial as they are varied and yet one thing seems ominously certain. Headteachers in particular will not be able to achieve everything single-handed. One essential leadership quality will be the capacity to delegate sensibly. Empowering colleagues with authority and responsibility can, and should, no longer be viewed as an abrogation of duty. It is better viewed as a creative opportunism, an offer of faith and trust, a sentiment of belief in the abilities of one's staff. We must, obviously, be aware of potential pitfalls. We should avoid overburdening those who inveterately volunteer for everything. We must be certain that an individual is really able to fulfil the expectations demanded of him or her and we must be on our guard against those who view additional responsibility as callous, authoritative malice.

Our current working environment will impel us to share responsibilities in schools, to renegotiate job descriptions at regular intervals and to re-assess workloads. We must allow leaders to emerge within a structure that, through teamwork, develops a hierarchy of its own making. Personal respect is at the core of this, yet respect is earned, not granted, in schools. Senior management must examine the staffing structure, negotiate new or changed roles, delegate responsibilities, lead by example and as circumstances alter over time, keep the whole process under review. A tighter job market may gradually reduce movement between schools, but the vagaries of funding and curriculum development suggest that regular changes may need to be contemplated from within.

External support

This evaluation of future personnel issues began by focusing on a staff development and welfare policy for one school. Having explored various institutional contexts, schools must also consider levels of external support. I am advocating that schools look inwardly if they wish to manage their own future. The continuing demise of local authorities has gradually reduced one level of influence over schools and, in so doing, exposed a deep chasm between need and provision. Some would argue that the ability of LEAs to selectively support schools was reminiscent of medieval patronage and beneficence. It was, however, one source of appeal that might fall on acquiescent and supportive ears. There was always the hope and possibility that an LEA might provide the required service or even financial support. We are now in what many non-educationalists lovingly describe as the 'real world', as they chuckle at the prospect of no more hand-outs, public sympathy and closeted security, as if these ever really existed. In coming to terms with this 'real world', schools will have to seek out the services and support they need and be prepared to pay for the privilege. Yet not all support comes with a price tag. There are the parents, the governors, the local community and an educational community that might willingly enter into some profitable form of symbiotic relationship. We must, therefore, seek to advance our cause by enlisting the support that *is* available. Parents can provide the additional pair of hands that makes life in the classroom less burdensome. Governors can gain increasing understanding of the school and provide support in a whole range of meaningful ways. Local people may sponsor your sports teams, allow you to use their facilities and speak up for your efforts. The list of possibilities is endless and most schools are fully aware of them.

The main lesson is, however, that schools cannot exist in isolation. Their very survival may depend upon precisely how they seek to harness the potential support available to them. Each of the above constituents may, and probably will, require policies devised collectively to ensure that links are established which provide continuity and progression. The cynics may remonstrate against more policy documents and time devoted to issues apparently outside the premises. Perhaps the cynics have not quite entered the 'real world' yet?

Legislative issues

If schools wholeheartedly prepare for the future by producing plans that operate on different levels, accounting for school development, staff development and staff welfare, then they have taken significant steps towards self-determination. It would be an unfortunate consequence of striving for a productive, supportive environment were excessive self-congratulation to result. Schools must celebrate their successes, but they must also beware the dangers of complacency. Just when you thought it was safe to go back in the water, something else appears on the horizon! For example, one important consideration arises from recent EC directives which place additional responsibilities upon schools. New sets of regulations will come into force which are more demanding yet perhaps offer a safer passage through a poorly charted sea of existing health and safety situations which are liberally splattered with reefs of regulations, rules and statutory requirements. Staff safety representatives will obviously have an important part to play in any genuine policy which has staff welfare at its heart.

One feature of leadership which is increasingly important is an innate ability to predict the future. The headteacher as soothsayer is a new, unwanted role which may have to be accommodated as schools seek to spot trends and developments. Divine prescience may be required as clues emerge and schools simply have to be prepared to interpret them. One such example relates to the requirement for schools to have 'Whole school pay policies'. They can provide a natural extension to staff development and welfare plans as they seek to focus on contracts, conditions of service and issues of pay. As schools throughout the country become increasingly familiar with full delegation, the various personnel functions that befall them may offer salutary premonitions of a less comfortable future without, perhaps, the legal and administrative base of an LEA to fall back on.

In order to offer staff security and to remain sensitive to an employer's duties and responsibilities, schools will need to produce a formal document or policy statement which clearly catalogues how various issues will be tackled. This could include appointments procedures, the interview process, promotion, resignation and redundancy, job specifications, job share provisions, rates of pay and policies relating to various increments and awards. The list might also include disciplinary and grievance procedures, definitions of expectations and responsibilities, indeed any area that helps to explain the legal framework in which a colleague (teaching or support) works.

As schools enter a period when temporary contracts will be used as a stop-gap measure and a safety valve rolled into one, they run the risk of being obsessed by contracts and short-term solutions to staffing difficulties. Equally, the spectre of performance related pay (PRP), the fear that appraisal will be linked with performance and hence with pay is inherently problematic. Studies suggest that there is no correlation between the use of performance-related pay and high performance although there are some indications that PRP may help to raise staff awareness of the importance of outcomes and service delivery standards and, therefore, could be effective as a spur to organisational improvement. Such benefits are more applicable to the business world than to schools, however, and it is not unreasonable to suggest that PRP is likely to motivate 20 per cent of employees at the expense of the remaining 80 per cent.

In addition, the obvious dichotomy which schools face between employing the best or the cheapest available teacher is not an encouraging scenario for those who were prepared to accept the trials of the classroom because they felt they had an element of so-called job security. The very word 'redundancy' is enough to strike fear into the most able and confident teacher, particularly when one's salary rather than one's performance could be the guiding factor when teachers' jobs are at stake. The preparation of a whole-school pay policy at least offers a set of agreed principles and structures that may underpin future staffing policy.

Ideally, such a document should be devised collaboratively and involve governors, teaching and non-teaching staff as well as senior management. This seems to be all the more appropriate if grant-maintained status is under consideration.

Ideally, consultation with the professional associations is sensible at such times and their involvement in policy making is more likely to result in support rather than suspicion when and if future difficulties do arise. This whole area of relationships with unions may become more tightly focused as schools seek to deal with situations without the benefit of LEA intermediaries. The final policy might take into account the status of unions within the school so that everyone is clear about due process and procedure.

The maxim 'knowledge is power' seems entirely appropriate for this particular aspect of staff management and deployment. All staff really do need to have access to information and clearly defined responsibilities. Uncertainty can lead to stress, particularly if staff are ambiguous about what is expected of them. Colleagues will increasingly require a regularly reviewed and updated 'information file' which goes beyond wet playtime procedures and actually provides an interpretation of conditions of service as they apply specifically to the school. This might be the result of a further collaborative venture which could prove to be an invaluable awareness-raising exercise. The various contents of such documents could be as diverse as colleagues feel necessary but should certainly interpret matters which directly affect staff, such as directed time allocations, supervision requirements and health and safety matters. Governor approval of or participation in the preparation will lend validity and importance to a document that can serve as a crucial reference point for the future.

Information documents are not the sole prerogative of teachers. They can be usefully prepared for support staff, students and governors so that a unitary school information document underpins personnel management in the school.

As management tools, pay policies and information booklets, if carefully assembled, can sit comfortably alongside staff development and welfare plans contributing to a whole school commitment to openness, honesty and clarity. These are ideals which are intrinsically worthwhile but also help to create the managerial climate that is desirable for continuity and progress during the next few difficult years. That climate will be easier to maintain if governors are supportive, yet the response and reaction of governors to their personnel function is difficult to gauge accurately. For example, horror stories abound of governors seeking to dismiss staff without reference to legal processes. At the other extreme, there is evidence to suggest that many governors feel unprepared for and confused by the sheer range of their powers. Governors may, therefore, remain an unknown quantity, but not one which can be ignored. They will need to be guided, supported, involved and often obeyed. The actual quality and scale of staff development may depend upon governors' interest and reaction. A degree of optimism may be required, yet the best insurance policy is surely to be seen to be doing a good job as a result of the policies already in place.

The future is, therefore, unclear but certainly not hopeless. We will undoubtedly be seen increasingly as masters of our own fate and must respond accordingly. Despite the evidence of good practice which most schools can generate, no institution can afford to rest on its laurels. Being a caring school is no longer enough. SATS results and league tables put a halt to that. The exploratory discussion paper from Alexander, Rose and Woodhead (1992) clearly set new ground for debate in primary schools and its influence is likely to turn attention to the organisation, management and deployment of staff for years to come. It is difficult to envisage a future without controversy or a time when schools can pause for lengthy reflection. Yet opportunities will arise.

Much of the legislation which schools have encountered increases their isolation and insularity. Having recommended co-operation from within as an essential means for staff to cope with the various pressures, it seems entirely sensible for schools to co-operate with one another for the mutual benefits that this can engender. Schools do not *have* to compete, despite the encouragement to do so. They can still learn from each other, share expertise and even work together if they have a mind to do so. Staff have always exchanged ideas informally and benefited from the process. Why not formalise the process? All that is required is the will and commitment of those involved, and heads and governors in particular. A big question mark clearly hangs over this suggestion but if the benefits are emphasised and responsibilities shared, the dividends could be massive. This is probably an expression of hope rather than expectation, yet that is perhaps the best way to approach the future if we really are to give staff and children the schools they deserve.

In advocating a future based upon self-empowerment and self-determination, I must reinforce my belief in the need for optimism. The potentially destructive force of human apathy and inaction remains too great a threat to think otherwise.

References

Alexander, R. Rose, J. and Woodhead, C. (1992) 'Curriculum Organisation and Classroom Practice in Primary Schools: A Discussion Paper' DES.

Maslow, A. (1970) 'A theory of human motivation' *Psychological Review* **50**, pp.370–396.

OFSTED (1993) *The Handbook for the Inspection of Schools* HMSO.

6 Managing the external environment

Jane Startup and Linda Ellison

Introduction

Managing the external environment is a key aspect of primary school management. The osmosis between the school and its environment requires skilful management of both the internal and external aspects of the school, yet many headteachers have approached this in an ad hoc way. Schools have always had to deal with parents, governors and the local community but now a more carefully planned approach is required to managing the links with a wide range of groups such as those shown in Figure 6.1.

It is now more difficult to identify the boundaries of the school and, hence to categorise groups into those which are internal and those which are external. For example, the governors carry most of the ultimate responsibility for the school's activity, the parents support their children in their learning, local industry and the Training and Enterprise Council may provide support with staff development and the secondary schools may supply some curricular expertise. It would therefore be more accurate to consider this chapter to be concerned with managing at the boundaries as well as managing the external environment.

Up until recently, most schools were controlled by local education authorities, with visits from Her Majesty's Inspectorate (HMI)

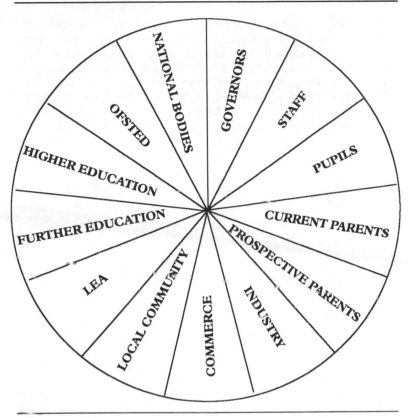

Figure 6.1 Internal and external groups and organisations

being few and far between. Now schools are facing a changing relationship with LEAs and every school is awaiting a visit from OFSTED every four years. The DfE and the School Curriculum and Assessment Authority (SCAA) exert a continuous influence upon the life and management of all primary schools. The amount of paperwork generated from them has placed great demands on each headteacher's management skills and stress levels. They have changed by law, the role and accountability of all headteachers.

In order to meet these changes effectively, it is important for headteachers to be proactive and to anticipate trends and demands. They need to pay more attention to external factors which affect the school and actively to promote the school's image. If they are to discover how people outside the school perceive it, headteachers need to listen and be seen to act upon people's views. In developing good practice, the headteacher needs to encourage co-operation and

support both in the staff-room and in the wider community. By
using a collaborative approach, schools can raise the expectations
of all concerned and engender mutual respect and celebration of the
school's achievements. As more schools take on board the idea of
'total quality management', then 'meeting the customers' needs' and
'getting the right things right, first time' becomes a way of life.

This chapter considers some of the many aspects of managing
the external environment or managing at the boundaries, focusing
in particular on:

• governors;
• parents;
• other educational institutions;
• the LEA;
• the local community; and
• the media.

Managing the relationship with governors

Governors' roles and responsibilities have greatly increased during
the past eight years. Their wide-ranging powers and responsibilities
make it essential for a school to establish a strong and positive links
with the governing body. It is the job of the headteacher to manage
the development of this relationship, enabling governors to become
more effective in their role.

Central to this issue is the working relationship between the
headteacher and the chair of governors. It is necessary for strong
support, mutual respect and an efficient administration system on
both sides. Both headteacher and the chair of governors must be
open and honest with one another. They will need to establish
regular communications, by phone or fax, and by visits to the
school. In that way, the chair of governors will have an overview
of how the school is being run, whilst leaving its actual day-to-day
management to the headteacher. It is important that these different
roles are understood by all concerned.

It is important that good working relationships are established
between all the governors, the headteacher and the staff. Praise and
encouragement should be articulated between each of the parties as
it makes people feel valued and supported. All governors can play
an active role in overviewing the management of the school. Every
governor should be made aware of the school's mission statement, its
long-term and short-term aims. It is the headteacher's responsibility
to enable governors to take an active part in the planning process
of the school and to be aware of the implications of financial
planning.

The daunting role of the school governor can be tackled more easily if there are working parties or sub-committees which report back to the meeting of the full governing body. Many schools have working parties or sub-committees to cover curriculum, personnel, premises and finance. Governors should be aware of the implementation of the school development plan and help in evaluating the outcomes each year. The governing body has responsibility for specific parts of the curriculum — e.g. religious education, health and sex education. They should also be aware of the school's policy and strategies for dealing with children who have special educational needs. These areas could be addressed through the governors' curriculum group or governors could nominate a particular governor to carry that responsibility.

Governors can be encouraged to play an active role in the life of the school and to understand the issues faced by the staff and pupils on a day-to-day basis. Strategies which schools have used include nominating 'a governor of the month' when one governor is responsible for visiting the school, liaising with the headteacher and staff, and dealing with the governors' post bag. Some larger schools link a governor with a class, which becomes their special responsibility. Some governors can also be invited to be present at parents' evenings so that they have an informal opportunity to meet the parents. This role usually falls to the parent governors but it may be more appropriate for others to be present; after all, the parent governors are already very closely in touch with the views and concerns of parents and are probably well known to many 'at the school gate'.

Even before the Education Reform Act, school governors' meetings were the source of many tales of late night meetings with agendas containing many items which seemed to have little connection to the learning needs of children. The amount of work to be covered demands tight management of the meetings. Headteachers should ensure that consultation takes place between the clerk to the governors and the chair of the governors well before the agenda is set. If possible, the agenda should include a 'time budget' — precise allocation of time for each agenda item. The headteacher's report to governors should be sent out with the agenda as well as any other appropriate documents, at least seven days before the meeting. At the meeting itself, it is advisable for the chair of governors, the headteacher and the clerk to sit near to one another so that informal communication is easy! Minutes of the meeting should be kept as brief as possible, whilst making clear who has responsibility for any tasks to be completed. Effective structuring and chairing of the meeting are important for a variety of reasons. Firstly, it gives a positive image of the education system to those from a wider background such as industry and commerce. Secondly, it prevents some people from pursuing their own 'agendas' which may not always be in the best interests of the school. Thirdly, good management of the meeting will prevent it from running for too long, thereby making effective use of time and preventing resignations from those in the community who have a lot of experience to offer but have limited time at the school's disposal.

The governors' annual general meeting (AGM) for parents needs to be organised in much the same way, the only difference being the issue of who writes the report to be presented to the parents. Officially, it is the job of the chair of governors but headteachers often find themselves asked to do this task. It is up to individual schools to negotiate the role. It would appear that the great majority of parents are not attracted to the governors' AGM and schools have tried various ideas to entice parents to attend — cheese and wine social evenings, performances by the school choir, or a discussion, with videos, on teaching sex education! Headteachers are still unsure whether to be disappointed at poor turnouts or simply relieved that parents have little to raise and are, presumably satisfied with the school's performance.

One of the newest legal responsibilities placed upon governors is that of the OFSTED inspection. It is the responsibility of the governing body to provide information to the registered inspector before the inspection, to prepare the school action plan after the inspection and to report back to parents on any action being taken. Until all schools have been through this exercise, both governors and staff will be uncertain and will look for support and training.

Training for governors, which is partially funded through specific grants, is provided by LEAs, higher education institutions or education consultants. Governing bodies may also like to consider joining a national body, such as the National Association of Governors and Managers (NAGM) or Action for Governors Information and Training (AGIT) which provide regular newsletters and helplines as well as training opportunities and conferences. Value-for-money should be a priority when deciding upon governor training. What has often been lacking to date is a clear view of the training needs of individual governors and, in particular, of the governing body as a whole. This will allow for a realistic assessment of the appropriateness of the training opportunities which are offered. For some needs, it may be more appropriate for someone to work with the whole governing body, rather than send a few people on a course. As well as external consultants in the usual sense, this may be a member of the school staff or there could be reciprocal arrangements with other schools so that a broader perspective is gained.

Managing the relationship with parents

If a school is to provide effective education for its pupils, it is important that there are positive partnerships with parents and that the relationship is managed in a pro-active way. There is now the added dimension of accountability to the public and this reinforces the need to ensure good relationships and communication with parents. For example, the Parents' Charter and the emphasis on parental choice in the Education Reform Act (DES 1988) has given parents a greater awareness of their rights and responsibilities. OFSTED inspections will assess 'how well parents are informed and served by the school, and contribute to its life' (Section 7.8)

Many schools have welcomed parents into school and they have provided practical support in the classroom — hearing children read, baking, visiting local libraries and so on. Fewer schools have considered using parents as volunteer helpers for administrative tasks yet this is an area where teachers spend far too much of their valuable time, moving pieces of paper from one file to another. As schools move towards more sophisticated computerised administration systems, the demand for paper accountability may reduce. However, for many, a helping hand with the sea of paper-work, from a reliable volunteer, would provide welcome support.

Parent–teacher associations are well-established in many schools while others have tried to broaden the concept by including members of the local community in 'friends of the school' groups. Such groups can add much to the life of the school, for example by organising social and/or fund-raising events. Schools usually rely on a small core of parents to run these groups, which can be advantageous as there is a need to deal directly with only a few people. On the other hand, it is important to be aware of the disadvantages: do the events organised appeal to a large cross-section of parents or is there a danger of appealing to a small clique? Are events which are organised to raise funds doing just that: if such an event raises less than £100 is it worthwhile in terms of the effort involved? Questions such as these draw attention to the need to be clear about objectives, even when organising activities beyond the formal curriculum, especially when there is extensive commitment of teachers' time.

Most primary schools have involved parents in helping their children at home, particularly with reading. Early years teachers have been very successful in involving parents with early mathematical and pre-reading skills, as well as enhancing the necessary social skills. But how does a school encourage the less-enthusiastic parents to be actively involved in their children's on-going education? Home visits may be one way to promote greater understanding between parents and school. Those schools which have not already done so may consider appointing a co-ordinator for home-school liaison. This teacher could oversee the development of a whole-school approach to parent–school links. One important aspect of this relationship is for schools to recognise the pool of expertise and talent which parents and grandparents possess — and use it to their advantage! Local historians, knitters, spinners, joiners, brickies and nurses are all out there, waiting to be invited into school to share their special talents.

A major aspect of parent–school relationships is that of communication, both formal and informal. Do parents feel at ease when visiting the school? How welcoming is the entrance hall? Do they feel able to talk freely to staff, both teaching and support? Does the school operate an 'open-door' policy? School ethos will determine how relationships form and develop. More formal occasions demand careful management, in terms of staff involved, time allocated, rooms and equipment used. What is more difficult to manage is the development of an open, friendly and approachable attitude in school staff. Whatever the occasion — parent interviews, open days, workshops for parents — the key to success is a well-managed environment with caring, interested staff.

Written communications from school give parents hidden messages as well as the intended information. Are reports, newsletters and school brochures well-presented? If hand-written school reports are sent to parents are they legible as well as being precise and informative? Some of the key points in relation to written communications such as newsletters and prospectuses are summarised below. A group of parents may cast a helpful eye over draft documents.

1. Decide on the purpose — is it for future reference, for short term use, for marketing?
2. Decide on the key issues to be communicated.
3. Documents should be simple, eye catching and tasteful. A cluttered document loses its impact. Bold headings and concise text broken up are better than large pieces of dense text.
4. Have the reader in mind. Is the language used appropriate for its audience, rather than full of jargon? Are sentences kept to a minimum length? Often a second person can make alterations to a document which make it considerably shorter and simpler without losing any meaning. It is important, however, that the

sentence and paragraph structure does not become so simple as to insult the intelligence of the reader.

5. Where appropriate, use high quality pictures and diagrams as these help to keep people reading and looking!
6. Do not make the document too long. As well as adding to the expense, effectiveness is often lost.
7. Include a contact number and name.

The quality of documentation, in relation to content and presentation, is of paramount importance and it is worth investing time in developing the school's written communications.

So far, the management of parent–school relationships has been considered from the school's point of view. In these days of 'customers' and 'clients' it is important that schools have sufficient information about the requirements of parents. How does a school seek parents' views? Having gained this information, how do schools develop an understanding of parents' views? As more schools use the development planning cycle, review and evaluation of all aspects of the school become part of everyday life. Why not extend the review and evaluation exercise to parents? Parents can be asked directly after meetings, or can be asked to fill in a short response form on the end of the newsletter. Carefully researched questionnaires can be sent out to parents on specific issues. With the information received, schools can celebrate their achievements and react to any criticism. Thus schools can actively manage their reputation. The information gathered will also provide useful evidence for presentation to OFSTED inspectors.

Schools will have to consider and overcome any practical difficulties which may arise because of the building or the people involved. How is a school to 'absorb' parents? Do the staff welcome visitors in the staff-room? Are there enough seats in there? Are parent helpers aware of the need for discretion and confidentiality? Who is to train parent volunteers to behave in an appropriate manner and how can the busy classroom teacher ensure that the parents are used to best effect? What does a school do in the case of the parents whose children are unhappy at home and who come to school to seek sanctuary in a secure and happy environment? If schools are actively seeking to improve the quality of parental support and encourage equality of opportunity for all parents to participate, they will have to plan to overcome any difficulties and to reap the rewards.

Managing the relationship with other educational institutions

Collaboration and good communication between educational institutions can benefit all concerned. Most significantly, it will improve continuity and progression for the learner but also it can allow for the more efficient use of resources and for the professional development of staff. Until recently, much of this communication was informal and depended on individuals building whatever links they felt were appropriate. Current funding mechanisms and the associated pressure on pupil and student numbers have meant that, in all phases of education, a more formalised process is needed with clear guidelines about collaboration.

Lack of money, together with a tradition of a collaborative approach in the primary sector has encouraged schools to work together. Often, cross-phase cluster groups (sometimes known as pyramids or families) have been actively supported by LEA funds. While there is still encouragement of the principle, LEAs have less money and some schools are grant-maintained so there is now a need to build resources into the individual school budgets. If these relationships are to survive in the more competitive climate, there will need to be forward planning and commitment to the scheme.

Cluster groups can provide a forum for passing information and ideas between the schools and the LEA or the DfE. The support can be a two-way process and can influence future decisions on both sides. Other examples of collaborative projects (some of which have previously been provided by LEAs) would be:

- sharing a technician, e.g. for information technology;
- inservice training and advice for curricular and management areas;
- evaluation of publishers' schemes e.g. for mathematics;
- sharing someone to maintain the school grounds or to carry out minor premises repairs;
- curriculum projects;
- teacher and pupil exchanges;
- sharing of expensive equipment.

In very small schools, close collaboration with others can allow for the formation of more viable groups of a similar age for such activities as team games and day or residential visits.

One of the problems arising from open enrolment and parental choice has been the fact that the pupils in one class may be transferring to several secondary schools. The problem is just as acute from the secondary schools' point of view. At least one school in England takes pupils from 70 different primary schools! Another result of the reforms is that there is some reluctance to form links in case other schools feel that this is favouritism or poaching. There are several reasons why, for the benefit of pupils, headteachers must try to overcome any political barriers and strengthen links with the appropriate secondary schools:

- parents will have confidence in the continuity of the educational process;
- pupils will not experience curriculum overlap;
- pupils will continue to progress: there has been evidence that pupils go back several months when they move on to secondary school and much of this can be attributed to lack of information about the curriculum covered, rather than to social factors;
- approaches to teaching and learning can be co–ordinated across the changeover; pupils in the primary school have been encouraged to be independent learners and users of resources but the organisation of a secondary school and the nature of much of the teaching fails to build on this in the early stages;
- pupils will feel comfortable about changing schools, a process which may cause them to be separated from their friends and which is a culture shock in that the secondary school is usually so much bigger and the child moves from being amongst the oldest in the school to being amongst the youngest.

Teacher exchanges are now becoming more frequent as is the practice of specialist teachers from secondary schools being used to run staff development workshops for primary colleagues. One possibility which could strengthen curricular links and help the pupils to feel more relaxed is for the primary teacher to take pupils to use the secondary school's facilities e.g. science laboratories. This requires considerable advance planning so that appropriate topics are left until the space is available – normally in the summer.

The building of relationships with colleges of further education is also beginning to occur. One tertiary college (presumably with an eye to future recruitment) has organised a 'primary week' in the summer when pupils have full use of the college's facilities.

Primary schools have usually been very willing to offer placements to teaching practice students from higher education and the classroom teacher has taken the main role in overseeing the student's work. Now that there is a greater responsibility at the school level, headteachers and deputies are having a much more formal role. Headteachers are having to decide on the costs and benefits of being involved in the schemes offered by different higher education institutions. If the school's resources are not to be drained by being involved in the partnership, new management skills are required such as negotiation skills and the ability to weigh up costs and benefits with a degree of precision. Many schools and universities/colleges are extending the nature of the partnership by formulating a mutually beneficial 'package' to include initial teacher training, inservice courses, research and consultancy. An awareness of the political and funding environment is needed here so that schools can capitalise on the opportunities available.

Managing the relationship with the LEA

The role of the LEAs, indeed their very existence has been threatened by recent Education Acts and local government reforms. To date, the vast majority of schools have, however, decided to continue their relationship with their own LEA. The future shape and role of LEAs is uncertain. Whilst some schools may perceive this as a threat, others are seizing the opportunity to play a more positive role in the partnership. The service provided by LEAs is now more closely focused upon schools' needs and, as schools move towards a more equal partnership, LEAs are recognising the need to consult and work together on long-term planning. This development may cause tension between LEAs and grant-maintained schools in the future.

LEAs have always seen an important part of their role as offering support and advice. Now schools are 'consumers' and free to buy in support from elsewhere, LEAs have had to look very closely at the quality of service they provide. Certain legal duties, such as monitoring schools and reporting back to education committee members remain, as do the requirements to provide the resources necessary for special needs and transport. As schools receive a greater percentage of delegated money, then specific services such as personnel officers, legal officers and LMS officers are operating as stand-alone agencies within the LEA. Once schools have the money for these services delegated to them, they can buy in, as and when appropriate. This has already happened in the crucial area of LEA advisory and advisory teacher provision. In authorities where this service still exists, schools are able to plan their input, rather than pick from a menu of one-off courses previously on offer. School development planning has enabled schools to identify curriculum areas which need support — either by sending staff on courses or by inviting LEA staff to work in school. In this way each school's specific needs can be targeted and appropriate strategies used. Schools are in the powerful position of stating who, when, how and where the input will take place.

Staff development and staff appraisal, if linked to the school development plan, can be positively supported by LEA inspectors and advisers. Judicious use of specific funding can enhance staff development. However, all schools are aware that the GEST funding is inadequate and inequable. Nursery and reception class teachers are not funded, and as GEST money is directed at specific government initiatives, certain subjects, particularly the arts, tend not to be funded adequately. Support staff receive no funding for staff development, yet if their role is to expand and develop, it is essential. Schools need to address these issues and find extra funds from within their budgets to support these areas. Only then can they buy in the appropriate expertise.

Both LEAs and schools are concerned with providing a high quality education which is economic, efficient, effective and equitable. Both sides are aware of the need for resource planning and development planning to be interdependent. This can only move forward if all schools and LEAs are actively involved in the planning cycle: audit, plan, implement and review. In addition, the information needs of the schools should be considered. If they are to operate effectively, they need accurate, up-to-date information which is not always available, especially in relation to the budget.

If both schools and LEAs are pro-active in managing their changing relationship, a culture of partnership will establish a new climate for decision taking and a shared commitment to change.

Managing the relationship with the local community

It is important for schools to know their standing and reputation in the local community. Then they know where they need to direct their attention in building and maintaining relationships with that community.

A school should be responsive to the character and culture of the local community, actively working to build links. Of course, a school is involved with the local community in the sense that it provides education predominantly for local children, although some schools provide education for others from the community. All primary schools use the local environment in their studies and many schools invite local people into school to share their skills and expertise.

Children play an active role in the community, often joining local clubs and societies such as Brownies or Boys Brigade. Staff members may also be involved, especially if they live in the local community. Schools often host activities after school closes and the DfE is actively encouraging an extension of this in the area of after-school activities and child-care facilities according to the needs of the local community. In order to forge strong links with individuals and organisations in the local community, good communications to and from the school are essential. Many schools provide work experience placements for secondary school or college students. A few schools have used the teacher placement service to enable a staff member to experience a different aspect of the world of work. As part of the cross-curricular themes, all schools will need to address 'economic awareness'. Good links between the school and local industry and commerce will help to develop this area of the curriculum.

Much good work done in schools may not be recognised by members of the public because of national perceptions about the state of education. Schools need to celebrate and publicise their achievements. This should be planned rather than allowed to develop on an ad hoc basis. It is not enough for a school to be successful, it must also be seen to be successful. In order to communicate this success to the local community, schools must adopt a positive approach to public relations and marketing the school.

Managing the relationship with the media

Local and national media can be very significant in conveying messages about individual schools and about the education service in general. With careful planning and management, schools can use this power to maintain a positive image in the wider community and also to allow pupils to gain recognition for their activities. Individual primary schools are most likely to achieve this through the local press although regional television and radio features may be possible if the school has achieved something unusual which is of interest to the general public.

It takes time to build relationships with the media so it is usually desirable to designate a member of staff who will be responsible for this. Some schools are lucky enough to have a member of staff or a governor with a media background who knows how best to maximise the school's potential in this area. Primary schools often complain because they have invited the local press to attend an event but no one appears. It is better to build links and to discover the best way of having material included in a paper or a programme. Usually the school needs to provide a photograph and a press release which should be relatively concise and should be compiled with some understanding of what will gain and retain the reader's interest.

It is most important that the school has a policy on dealing with any 'bad news' which may arise. In this case all staff need to be aware of how to deal with enquiries but normally the headteacher should be the person who provides the formal response. This is emphasised by Davies and Ellison:

> It should be made clear to all staff that, under no circumstances, do they make comments on behalf of the school, however innocent the question seems. At critical times it is important that a consistent balanced view is expressed and that the press are not given the opportunity to exploit a number of ill thought-out responses. It is always worth remembering that newspapers exist to sell copies and not necessarily to protect the reputation of schools!' (Davies and Ellison 1991, p.115).

Conclusion

Schools exist in a rapidly changing environment. Partnerships which are very strong and very significant one year may be much less so twelve months later. New relationships, often requiring different skills, must be built and maintained if the school is to provide the best possible experience for its pupils. Headteachers need to be aware of the changes which affect schools but they must prioritise the use of time and must involve others, such as parents, pupils, staff and governors in the management of external relations.

References

DES (1988) *Education Reform Act* IIMSO.
Davies, B. and Ellison, L. (1991) *Marketing the Secondary School* Harlow: Longman.

7 Managing the primary school budget

Max Amesbury

Introduction

Trying to manage the primary school budget often reminds me of that oft used saying 'you can't get a quart out of a pint pot'. In the days when schools only had to manage capitation there were many in the profession who complained that there just was not enough money to buy the textbooks, display paper, scissors and so on that the school needed. Now, of course, the same argument is being applied to the cost of electricity, cleaning staff, experienced teachers, repairing broken windows and insurance. And it does not end there — there is the problem of finding the time to deal with all of the above. This, in turn, entails trying to balance the conflicting demands on time — weighing the demands of giving quality time to children and staff against obtaining quotes for repairs, interviewing staff for a vacant cleaning post and shopping around for reasonable insurance cover.

To the initiated it all sounds reassuringly depressing. Reassuring because at least I know that the vast majority of budget managers are in the same boat, or at least captaining similar boats. What often happens in a situation of this sort (and this is particularly true of education) is that we, the professionals, sail around in circles without passing on to others some of the experience gained whilst negotiating rough seas.

The art (or is it a science?) of managing the primary school budget and of getting a quart out of a pint pot demands two personal qualities. The first is flexibility. If one method of operating a section of the budget is not successful then, after a time, try another but beware of knee jerk reactions. The second quality is to be the eternal optimist and to say to yourself 'soon the Government is going to realise that we have been doing a grand job under very difficult circumstances and as a reward they are going to fill up that quart pot until it is overflowing'!

In this chapter I intend to highlight a number of areas connected with the budget within which I hope to give some useful advice, offer a range of options or just admit that there is no apparent simple answer. All, or almost all, are based on my experience as a headteacher of two very different schools and as chair of governors of another, over the last six years.

The budgetary cycle

The school budget is the means of relating expenditure to educational need. Before discussing some practical aspects of the primary school budget, it is necessary to consider the budgetary process which provides the decision-making framework. The budgetary element of a management cycle can be seen as a cycle of activity comprising four stages: budgetary review, budgetary forecasting, budgetary implementation and budgetary evaluation (see Figure 7.1).

I have included a section from Davies (1994) which I consider relevant as it describes in some detail the component parts of this cycle.

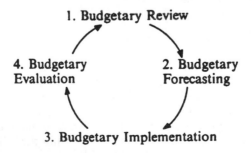

1. Budgetary Review

4. Budgetary
Evaluation

2. Budgetary
Forecasting

3. Budgetary Implementation

Figure 7.1 The budgetary cycle

1. Budgetary Review

This first stage of the budgetary cycle involves an assessment of the current financial position of the institution and the underlying causal factors. This review has two elements to it. One is a check of current levels of income and expenditure in key categories such as:

Income

- Funds from funding formula linked to pupil numbers
- Funds from pupil charges
- Funds from specific bidding projects/ categories
- Community-based financial support
- Income from investments
- Income from lettings

Expenditure

- Staffing
- Premises-related expenses
- Curriculum-related expenses
- Organisation-related expenses

Once current levels of income and expenditure have been checked, the managers in the institution should move on to the second element of the audit and ask some fundamental management questions:

- Is the institution balancing its income and expenditure?
- Are there significant levels of over or underspending in particular areas?
- Can financial resources be reallocated (vired) from one area to another to increase educational outputs or organisational efficiency?

2. Budgetary forecasting

Having assessed the current position, it is important that in the second stage, before the design and implementation of the new budget takes place, the impact of likely future financial trends is assessed to set any financial decisions in context. This is a significant activity which is new to many educational managers as, traditionally, budgeting within the education sector has taken place on an annual basis. It is now necessary to examine the impact of financial decisions and the general resource environment over a longer period to establish a multi-year-time-horizon (MYTH) to provide this context.

In a resource-constrained environment educational organisations struggle to achieve their objectives while keeping their educational income and expenditure in balance. It is a mistake to view budgetary decisions within a one-year time-frame. There are several examples that illustrate this. One would be the adoption of learning schemes that use a workbook approach and thus have considerable future material costs. Another would be a planned replacement of computers over time. In the staffing field, an example is provided by choosing between two members of staff where the initial difference in salary (owing to the point on the salary spine) of £7,000 can, over a five-year period cost in the region of £35,000 depending on progress up the salary spine.

Another key management factor in the budgetary forecasting context is whether the institution has an increasing or decreasing resource base and the relationship of that to the budget balance. If the pupil population is increasing then, on formula-based funding, a positive financial framework will be created. This can overcome any marginal overspending in the current budget. This longer-term perspective is necessary before the manager takes action to adjust the current budget otherwise unnecessary cutbacks may be made. Conversely, if the institution is facing declining numbers, owing to either increased competition or demographic factors or both, then remedial action on the budget needs to be taken promptly or the deficit will get out of hand. The following provides a useful checklist of factors that should be included in a financial forecasting exercise:

- Pupil roll.
- Changes in the make-up of the overall roll — more older/younger pupils with their different formula weightings would affect the budget.
- Changes in the formula-funding mechanism either by the LEA or the central government funding agency.
- Projections of extra support funds i.e. gifts, donations (PTAs etc), income from lettings.
- Projections of success in bidding for specific central government or private sector grants.
- Costs of extent of staffing changes, retirements, movement up the pay spine and their subsequent financial implementations.
- Costs of new curricula or predictable replacement costs for learning schemes.

- Costs of essential maintenance cycle.
- Planned expansion/contraction costs re capital and revenue.
- New sources of income identified or additional areas of necessary expenditure.

When this context has been set then the next stage, budgetary implementation, can be undertaken.

3. Budgetary implementation

When drawing up the annual budget, reference back to the previous two stages needs to take place in order to set current decisions in the context of both the audit and future projections. A useful staged implementation process could be:

- Set out headings and sub-headings of the budget.
- Allocate fixed costs to headings.
- Allocate recurrent costs.
- Bring forward items from the audit and forecast stages to establish a priority list for available expenditure.
- Decide between alternative projects and courses of action.
- Put budget forward for approval by the institution's governors.
- Set check points during the year for possible virement opportunities.

It has to be appreciated that, even at this stage, as with all financial statements, this is a snapshot at a particular moment in time and that adjustments will have to take place as events unfold. Finally, the cycle moves on to the evaluation stage.

4. Budgetary evaluation

It is important that institutions do not ignore this vital stage of the budgetary process which can be split into two parts, one concerned with outcomes and one with process. The evaluation of outcomes must involve a consideration of how well the resource allocation decisions have enabled the institution to meet its objectives in an effective but also efficient way. The questions to be asked might be: did we achieve what we wanted? Was the money well spent? Would alternatives have given us a better use of resources?

As well as evaluating the output of the budgetary process

it is necessary to evaluate the process itself and the role of the people involved. Davies and Ellison (1992) provide a useful list:

- Who is involved in the budgetary process?
- What are the roles and responsibilities of governors, staff and parents? To what extent are they consulted or take part in the decision-making process?
- How is the review to be structured?
- Is the resourcing of certain areas to be examined in more depth on an occasional basis?
- Who is to summarise the review information, indicating priorities?
- When is the summary to be presented to the Governing Body?
- Who is involved with making forecasts?
- Who provides the data?
- Who makes final decisions about choices and allocations?
- Are these decisions based on the priorities identified in the school development plan?"

Having reviewed the nature of the budgetary cycle, the next step is to consider key areas in connection with the budget. Figure 7.3 shows the headings under which my current school budget is grouped. These categories will be used to structure

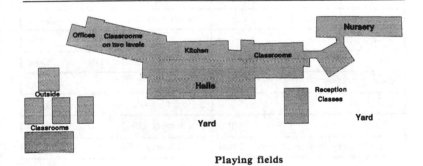

Playing fields

Statistics:-

Pupils   =   505 + 26 place nursery
Staff   =   Head + 21 teaching staff
               20 ancillary secretaries, lunchtime supervisors and assistants,
               nursery nurses and special needs assistants.
               1 caretaker
               (school 'buys in' cleaning, kitchen and grounds maintenance staff)
Classes   =   19 + nursery

Figure 7.2   The school site and structure

BUDGET HEADING		BUDGET HEADING	
Expenditure		*Expenditure Cont.*	
Staff Related Costs[1]		**Supplies & Services**[3]	
Teaching Staff	553300	Postage	300
Supply Cover	3000	Telephone	900
Officers	105300	Insurance - Supply Staff	10000
Manuals	13500	Insurance - Contents	2500
Total Staff Related Costs	**675100**	L.E.A. Services	2540
Premises Related[2]		Adult Canteen Meals	1500
Building & Maintenance	4000	Admission Charges	1850
Horticultural Maintenance	3020	Educational Visits	500
Cleaning	13700	Vehicle Costs	0
Toilet & Medical Supplies	600	Travel & Subsistence	100
Furniture & Fittings	2600	Recreational Transport	1320
Rents & Rates	18380	**Total Supplies & Services**	**21510**
Total Premises Related Costs	**42300**	**Financing Costs**	
Energy Related Costs		Leasing Charges	5450
Solid Fuel	0	Total Financing Charges	5450
Oil	5000	**TOTAL EXPENDITURE**	**786860**
Gas	1000	**Income**[4]	
Electricity	9500	School Meals Credit	-3200
Water	5000	Community Use	-5000
Total Energy Related Costs	**20500**	PSA Contributions	0
Capitation Costs		Insurance - Supply	0
Equipment & Materials	22000	Insurance - Contents	0
Total Capitation Costs	**22000**	Other Income -	0

Figure 7.3   School budget headings

BUDGET HEADING	BUDGET HEADING	
	Total Income	-8200
	Net expenditure	778660
	School Contingency	10000
	TOTAL ALLOCATION	788660
	Funding 94/95	786620
	Balance B/F 93/94	10000
	Safeguarding	4250
	TOTAL FUNDING	800870
	Surplus (+) / Deficit (-)	+ 12210

[1]Staff related costs
Officers - all ancillary staff i.e. secretaries, nursery nurses, special needs assistants and lunchtime supervisors and assistants.
Manuals - school superintendent / caretaker.

[2]Premises related costs
Cleaning - cleaners, refuse collection, window cleaning, cleaning equipment and materials.

[3]Supplies & Services
L.E.A. services - peripatetic music service.
Adult Canteen meals - staff who are intitled to a meal e.g. caretaker and lunchtime supervisory staff.
Admission Charges - sports centre, including swimming
Educational Visits - supporting those children who do not, or cannot make a voluntary contribution to trips.
Vehicle Costs - e.g. school mini-bus.
Travel & Subsistence - e.g. travelling expenses for attending governors' meetings.
Recreational Transport - e.g. transport to the sports centre.

[4]School Meals Credit - money back from the schools meals' service for the use of the kitchen.
Community Use - income from school lettings.

Figure 7.3   Continued

much of the remainder of this chapter but first I will consider
the school development plan as this provides the framework within
which the budget must operate. The six areas that follow later are
staffing, premises-related expenditure, energy-related expenditure,
capitation, insurance and income. In order to assist the reader,
details of the current school site and structure can be seen in
Figure 7.2.

The school development plan

Effectively managing the modern primary school is a team effort.
This entails the headteacher, senior staff, teaching staff and governors all working together. 'Perfect' in theory, but in practice
there are teachers and governors who do not want to 'co–operate'
with this approach. I suggest that this cannot be allowed to happen
and that the energies of the majority should be used to ensure
that what they decide is actually implemented. It depends almost
completely on a plan – and every school should have an effective
school development plan (SDP). The SDP, if managed correctly,
should allow all interested parties to have some input into its
construction. These interested parties include the headteacher and
all staff in the school, the governors and parents. I choose the order
in which I have listed these parties carefully. Other groups may also
have an influence including the local education authority (LEA),
the Department for Education (DfE), the Government (through its
legislation) and the OFSTED Inspectorate. The people who really
matter, however, in this team approach are the headteacher and
staff. Almost nothing of any real value or worth that is going to
affect the important work which goes on in school, that of educating
the children, can take place without the support of the staff. They
must endorse and have 'ownership' of any change which is planned
for the school. The headteacher is the facilitator of this change and
the governors are the overseers.

   As stated earlier, the budget needs to be looked upon within the
context of the school development plan. The needs of the school as
determined by the development plan drive the budget and therefore
its careful formulation is vital. SDPs come in all shapes and sizes
and the form that they take should be left to each individual school.
Nevertheless, there are certain elements which should be common to
all. Useful examples of practical development planning can be found
in Davies and Ellison (1992) and in Skelton, Reeves and Playfoot
(1991). Firstly, the plan should cover all aspects of the school, not
just the curriculum and staff development. Secondly, each 'plan'
will have its short-term and long-term targets. Short-term targets
are usually looked upon as those to be tackled within the next year

whilst the long-term targets are to be tackled within a two- to three-year period. Targets themselves need to be graded with a limited number of major short-term ones being prioritised. A manageable number might be no more than three or four. In addition to these major targets there are likely to be a considerable number of minor targets. Not all the targets have financial implications but many will, and they ought to be taken into consideration when planning the budget. Indeed, the costing of targets in the SDP is one of the factors which OFSTED inspectors take into account. Targets which are likely to require extra human resources, e.g. the employment of additional staff, must be carefully calculated. Major changes to certain areas of the curriculum can impose a large financial burden and must also be included such as replacing the school's current reading scheme. Other minor targets such as updating the school prospectus should not be too difficult to estimate. It is too easy to forget to include the time cost of such projects. Within the budget a separate heading can be provided for each priority or extra finance could be allocated to already defined budget areas. It could well be that some of the minor priorities may not be met within the short-term as planned. Experience has shown me that just as the SDP needs to be a flexible document, the budget too needs to have a degree of flexibility.

Because the budget and the SDP are inextricably linked it is unfortunate that the financial year and the academic year are not synchronised. Traditionally, budget decisions are taken either late in the spring term or early in the summer term. School development plans have tended to be discussed and decided upon in the summer term prior to the new academic year. In order to overcome this problem there seem to be two possible answers, although their adoption could demand quite a radical change in approach to planning by many primary schools.

(i) Start the school development plan in January

Apart from the New Year marking the start of the spring term, its passing almost goes unnoticed in schools. This could change significantly if it became the time of year when schools carried out their school development plan audit and prepared their targets for the year. This would fit neatly alongside the end of the financial year and the budget plans for the new financial year. This could be construed as the budget timing driving the SDP timing. Not so, but unfortunately it is fact that the end of the financial year is anchored in March. The same restrictions do not apply to the SDP except in our minds and therefore there is no reason why it cannot be moved.

(ii) Take a flexible approach to budget planning

Rather than restrict budget planning to a single year it is possible to plan over a longer period (a multi–year–time–horizon), such as three years. This approach could be particularly useful to schools when planning how to make best use of a surplus or when managing a deficit. Further mention of this type of planning will be made in the next section on staffing.

Staffing

Staffing, as all those involved in managing a school's finances are aware, consumes the vast majority of the total budget. Without doubt, however, it is any school's greatest asset and as such it must be carefully managed.

Many headteachers may look back nostalgically to those days when numbers of pupils in school started to rise and they picked up the phone to the LEA staffing division to argue the case for an extra member of staff. The same headteachers will probably smile about how slow they were to inform the staffing division about any fall in pupil numbers, hoping any 'surplus' members of staff may be forgotten about. Sadly, those days are long gone and staffing decisions, many of them difficult, are now taken by headteachers and governors.

Because employing staff entails the long-term commitment of large sums of money, in the early days of LMS schools appeared reluctant to take on staff whom in the old days they would have fought tooth and nail with the LEA to obtain. This was not altogether surprising since the whole business of LMS was new and no headteacher or governing body wanted to be carrying a deficit budget if they could avoid it. The result was that a considerable number of schools in those early days managed to achieve substantial cost savings which were translated into large surpluses at the end of the financial year. The concern amongst parents about large class sizes was probably ameliorated by the sight of painters and decorators busily covering up years of neglect or the appearance of a sudden influx of brand new computers into the school.

If the school has a budget deficit as a result of staffing 'problems' then this can be seen as a consequence of:

(a) a falling pupil roll and the resulting reduction in pupil- related income
(b) the school having a preponderance of experienced staff who are costly to employ because the 'formula', which determines the

amount of money each school receives, is based on average teacher costs.

During my time as headteacher and chair of governors I have seen both sides of the coin. In the first example, I was in the very pleasant position of dealing with a surplus. Over a relatively short period of time a number of staff appointments were made. Most of the teachers who were appointed were on less than average salaries and this ensured that, by the end of the financial year, the school had not used all its staffing budget. Even with a slight increase in the salary bill for the next year, it was obvious that there was money to spare. The staff were approached and asked whether they would prefer teacher help one day a week or help from an ancillary non-teaching assistant (NTA) for half a day every day. At the time, the cost of employing an NTA was approximately 40 per cent of the cost of employing a teacher. In this particular instance the teachers opted for the NTAs.

Savings on staffing may not always be sufficient to afford such regular support but forward planning should allow schools to think along the lines of extra provision during periods of increased pressure which occur during the school year. These may include that time of the year when SATs are in progress, Christmas activities are in full swing or pupil reports are being written. Forward planning of this nature can be included in the school development plan, thereby making teachers aware in advance that support will be available at certain busy times of the year.

Deficits are never so easy to manage although some have a relatively short-term solution. The following example is such a case. The number of children in our reception class created the need to employ another teacher. The budget which the school had been allocated for the year could not support employing another teacher. Parents were, at least, likely to protest at the situation or, at worst, decide to remove their children and send them elsewhere. Projected pupil figures for the next academic year were encouraging and this was a trend that should continue. By adopting the slightly risky strategy of employing a teacher now and carrying the deficit until the money was received for the extra pupils, it was considered that the crisis could be weathered. Schools, of course, are not used to being involved in the risk business and the adoption of longer-term budget planning is an alien approach for many.

One of the problems which schools often experience in connection with their financial position is that their final budget income may not be confirmed until well into the summer term. This makes it more difficult to plan for staff increases/decreases which may need to be made ready for the start of the new academic year. Again, this is a short-term problem which can be more ably managed by the adoption of a longer-term planning and budget strategy.

Dealing with a long-term staffing challenge, such as a wealth of experienced but expensive staff, demands that the school has to take an equally long-term budget strategy. Vacancies will occur from time to time and the majority of those posts will be for 'junior' positions and, as such, they are likely to attract candidates who will be employed initially on less than 'average' salaries. Although a long process, the situation should rectify itself as long as the school has a planned approach to maintaining a balanced staff.

From the early days of LMS, many schools have attempted to retain a percentage of staff on temporary contracts. This has allowed them to shed staff in times of financial difficulty and it is probably an option worth retaining although it is not without its drawbacks. Firstly, many staff on temporary contracts are likely to be looking for permanent posts and schools cannot assume that they have sole call on them. Secondly, telling temporary staff they no longer have a job in your school at the end of term or even that their hours are to be cut is never easy. It is important that all staff have a thorough understanding of the likely future roll of the school and of the staffing options which may be adopted. Handy (1989) refers to the need for organisations to be responsive to change and predicts that, more and more, staffing patterns will have a core of permanent staff and a periphery of temporary/part-time staff.

Premises–related expenditure

Within this section, I have chosen two areas which tend to absorb much time and money: buildings and cleaning.

Buildings

When managing the buildings, the tasks include obtaining quotations, deciding which quotation to accept, assessing whether the best value for money has been achieved and checking the finished job and quality of workmanship. These are the sort of decisions which we may expect to take in connection with our own homes but should the same tasks fall to the headteacher or other senior members of staff when alterations or repairs are needed to the school building? Parents would probably answer 'certainly not' but there is no doubt that such tasks have increasingly become part of the headteacher's job list. To reduce or remove the burden there is of course a cost implication. Below is a list of possible alternatives which is certainly not exhaustive but is based on personal experience except for the last which has been developed no further than the discussion stage:

(i) Use the LEA's building service (if it still has one) where LEA staff choose the contractor and will check on the quality of the workmanship, if asked, using their own surveyors. Main advantages — a complete service; no time wasted obtaining estimates. Main disadvantage — no real control over costs.

(ii) Send the caretaker on a 'handyman' training course so that s/he will be capable of tackling a wider range of jobs around school. S/he will not be able to tackle all the repairs required but the number which have to be contracted out will be reduced. Main advantages — repair costs cut; repairs can be carried out immediately; new development opportunity for the caretaker. Main disadvantages – s/he will require a comprehensive set of tools; allowances may have to be made for mistakes; care is needed with the legal liability aspects. Roles, responsibilities and remuneration will need to be reconsidered.

(iii) Employ a trained craftsperson/technician for a few hours per week. Main advantage — if a careful choice is made the person could have a wide range of skills and be capable of managing a wide variety of jobs around school. Main disadvantage — there is a shortage of skilled craftspeople willing to work for low wages; there may be some weeks s/he is not needed. It could also be possible to employ someone for more hours and to 'sell' services to the community or to operate a cluster arrangement with other schools.

(iv) Employ a surveyor amongst a cluster of schools to deal with obtaining quotes, offering contracts and quality control. Main advantage — a professional service provided. Main disadvantages — persuading other schools to agree; costs to be borne if some schools withdraw from the scheme.

(v) Co-opt a parent with building or surveying skills onto the governing body. Main advantage — free advice and contacts with other experts in the business. Main disadvantage — possible 'insider dealing' problems.

In the previous section, I mentioned the budget surpluses which often arise from savings being made on staffing and the fact that these are being used to carry out extensive painting and decorating. Upkeep and maintenance of the building would normally be funded from the buildings section of the budget and this can be designed to incorporate a planned programme of painting and decorating. As with other planned activities this programme can be written into the school development plan. Areas in need of decorating and which are the responsibility of the school can be placed in priority order with the intention, in the long run, of having a 5 to 10 year cycle involving the whole school.

The thorny question at the present time is that connected with the management of a capital building programme. Open enrolment may bring more pupils and therefore more money into schools but it does not bring sufficient to build permanent extensions to existing school buildings. The delegation of all centrally held LEA funds, particularly in connection with buildings, would not provide schools with sufficient to replace a boiler or to re-wire the whole school. A system of prioritising what needed doing in school would be of little value if the school was unable to meet the cost of those priorities. Long-term planning of two or three years is not appropriate here. Perhaps the only way is to allow schools to take out special LEA or government backed low interest loans. With so many schools in a very sorry state of repair this could be one of very few answers available.

Cleaning

In the early days of LMS, schools relied heavily on using the cleaning services set up by the LEA. This was not surprising since it was convenient, they had the labour, the expertise and were competitive on price. It was realised by schools within a very short time that the service provided by the LEA prior to compulsory competitive tendering was not the same once the new system came into force. In order to keep costs down the majority of schools found that the contractors cut staff or hours and, in some cases, both. The net result was that schools were not, in general, as clean as they had been. As a result there was a move by schools away from using the LEA services and towards the employment of private contractors or of their own cleaners. Of the three options the latter, in terms of quality of service, proved to be the most successful. Yet even this system has its drawbacks. Any problems associated with being the employer become the responsibility of the governors but in most cases the burden falls on the headteacher. Illness, recruitment and possible disputes are all potentially large consumers of time and we are back to the same old problem of measuring the best use of time against money. It must also be remembered that, in the case of this option, there is the added expense of purchasing and maintaining specialist cleaning equipment.

Nevertheless, the employment of their own cleaners is probably the road that many primary schools will prefer to take because the quality and the reduced cost of service outweigh the drawbacks.

For those who prefer the convenience of using the LEA services or those provided by an outside contractor, it is worth setting up a governors' sub-group onto which the caretaker can be invited. Their task could be to check the contract (and charges) on offer and to set up a system of quality control that does not involve senior management.

Energy related expenditure

A number of LEAs have realised that substantial savings can be made by careful management of energy and this, coupled with an 'in vogue' desire to be 'green', has caused them to set up energy efficiency units. Alternatively, there are many professional consultants advertising their services in this area of school management. Advice does not always follow the usual line of switching off lights when a room is not in use and keeping windows and doors closed, although this still needs to be part of any school's energy-saving strategies. The advice, as one would expect, does fall into two categories, short-term and long-term and some examples of each have been included in Table 7.1.

Day-to-day control of energy needs to be the responsibility of all members of staff, although reminding them of the need to support the school's energy-saving policy may be tedious and wearing. It is helpful if there is a written policy on the conservation of energy within the school and that everyone is aware of its contents, including the children. The caretaker/site manager can play a big part in regulating energy consumption, particularly over a period of twelve months, but s/he needs to establish a comprehensive system for checking timing controls and thermostats.

Some LEAs are now looking towards providing schools with loans for capital expenditure on schemes which, in the long run, will lead to reduced energy consumption. Finding out about such schemes is certainly worth the cost of a phone call.

LMS has proved a boon to plumbers' businesses as most schools have had more efficient urinal mechanisms installed. There is still scope for saving in this area if different taps are fitted so that they cannot be left running. The biggest saving has been made in some schools by changing the water meter to one which is more suited to the real demands of the school.

Table 7.1   Energy saving measures

Short-term	Long-term
Heating Check timing of heating clocks alongside occupancy. If there is a wide discrepancy, re-set. Check the system at least four times a year in line with the seasons. Adjustments should be made during the traditionally warmer times of the year or during periods of particularly mild weather to ensure that the system switches on later or, more likely, switches off earlier. Have 'special' settings for holiday periods when it is likely that only the cleaners will be in school. Set up a system of checking internal thermostat settings. Try to make them tamper-proof if possible.	*Heating* Replace old heating control clocks and thermostats with controls which provide greater flexibility and accuracy. Instal 'zone' controls which allow part of the building to be heated, particularly if community use is made of the premises. Replace electric fan or convector heaters with electric storage heaters or gas convector heaters.
Lighting Look towards replacing traditional lamps and bulbs (as they fail) with new energy-saving ones. If security lighting is on a time-clock, check and adjust at least four times a year in line with the hours of daylight.	*Lighting* Replace old lighting systems with new energy-saving systems.
General If electricity costs are high, check with the local electricity board to see if there is a cheaper tariff available. Ensure that all doors are self-closing (but not likely to trap fingers) and remove all door-holding catches. This is inconvenient at times but is definitely energy-saving.	*General* Check the energy consumption of the canteen freezers — it may be more than you think! Replace with new 'low energy consumption' freezers. Fit double doors to the outside. Instal extra insulation in roof and walls. Begin a rolling programme of fitting double-glazed windows (but consider the cost of vandalism).

Capitation

Perhaps 'capitation' is an outdated term for that parcel of money which headteachers have traditionally controlled to purchase the everyday items that the school needed, most of them consumables.

There will be many readers who will be able to relate stories about headteachers who treated capitation almost as if it were their own. They would spend hours ordering the stock and then hand parcels of it out to staff as if it was a birthday present. Others locked supplies away until the tubes of paint all went hard and only allowed staff to enter the Aladdin's cave under proper supervision, usually provided by the head, the deputy or the school secretary. In recent times many heads have allowed staff free access to all stock but have had great difficulty controlling the use of certain items, particularly pencils and white paint!

Many primary schools are now looking at alternative ways of dividing capitation. Secondary schools have traditionally asked department heads to be responsible for ordering resource materials to be used exclusively by their department. By using this method, staff are involved in the decision-making process of determining as individuals and as members of a team how this section of the budget should be spent. I offer the following method used by my school as an example. The scheme is in its infancy and small changes are likely to be made in the next few years as we learn from experience.

Last year, in preparation for the school development plan, staff were asked to complete a questionnaire covering almost everything to do with school and school life. The questionnaire highlighted the fact that teachers generally felt there was a need for more classroom resources. As a direct result of this, when the decisions about the next budget were being taken, each member of staff was allocated a sum of money from capitation to be spent on resources for his/her own classroom. The figures were weighted in favour of classes at either end of the age range. This was because nursery, reception and year 1 required large construction equipment whilst, as a 3–9 school becoming a 3–11 school, years 5 and 6 had to be set up with new equipment.

For some time the school had been operating a system whereby each year group in school received a certain amount of money to spend on necessities. This system has continued to operate although, during the coming year, the year groups are due to function in pairs (with reception joining years 1 and 2). The sum each 'pair' receives is based on the number of children in those year groups. This allows the year groups to purchase basics and resource materials for their topics. Topics are organised on a two year cycle so this approach re-enforces the team approach to planning and helps to promote continuity and progression.

Apart from a sum of money ear-marked for administration i.e. basic office requirements and photocopier paper, the rest is allocated to the curriculum areas. Curriculum spending is prioritised throughout the school development plan but there has to be sufficient money allocated to all curriculum areas in order to replace or buy certain basic resources including reading books and non-fiction library texts. All curriculum bids have to be listed in priority order and if the total amounts cannot be met out of the curriculum section of capitation then negotiations take place with each curriculum co–ordinator.

It is often better to lease some large items such as computers, photo-copiers and video cameras because the pace of technology is moving very quickly. Some leasing arrangements should be viewed with great suspicion but my school is particularly fortunate to be in a scheme organised through the LEA. The scheme has allowed the school to lease quite large quantities of expensive technical equipment over a three-year period. At the end of that time the school has the option of buying the equipment at a reduced rate from the leasing company but it has no obligation to do so. The very nature of the equipment means that it will be somewhat dated so the school will probably look towards signing another three-year leasing agreement to obtain more up-to-date equipment. Without such leasing schemes or the ability to spread the cost of buying expensive equipment, I suggest that it would be difficult for primary schools to keep pace with technology.

Insurance

As an example within this budget heading, I will discuss insurance to cover staff absence as it can be an expensive item. Many LEAs provide a staff absence insurance scheme for all their schools based on the average number of teacher absences across the authority. The result is a cost per teacher. A similar formula is applied to support staff. Schools with a history of high staff absenteeism can benefit financially from LEA insurance of this type, receiving back more than they pay into the scheme. Schools with good staff attendance are often not happy about this! Private insurance companies, of course, are unwilling to take on 'bad risk' schools but will provide a 'quote' per member of staff for those schools which they know to have a good staff attendance record. These companies offer the best premiums to those schools which are prepared to accept a two- , or preferably three-day absence excess before a claim is made. In practice, schools often find that staff absences do not generally last more than three days and, unless other arrangements are made, find themselves under pressure trying to cover internally. The possible alternative is to put more money into the staff supply section of the budget and less into supply insurance. Although insurance is still required to cover long-term absence, e.g. beyond five or seven days, premium charges should generally be lower. Schools need to budget for staff supply cover in a way that allows them most effectively to meet the needs of the school.

Income

Opportunities to create income are naturally limited but lettings are a source of revenue which may be worth investigating. It is important to have agreed with the governors a set of rates for the hire of parts of the premises such as classrooms, hall, playing fields. There then needs to be some room for negotiation available with would-be clients in order to remain competitive in the local area with, for example, community centres and church halls. As long as some lettings are within the caretaker's contract and he/she is not working outside these contracted hours, the cost of school lettings can be minimal, particularly to the aerobics group or during the warmer months when less heating is required! There are also relatively few costs involved in letting out the playground as a car park at weekends, a particularly good source of income for those near shopping centres.

Conclusion

There are a number of threads which are common to many of the areas that have been highlighted in this chapter:

(i) The budget plan should be an integral part of the SDP and should not be viewed as an 'add-on'.

(ii) The budget should be a tool serving the SDP and the whole of the school's needs in terms of finance.

(iii) Supporting the SDP is a team effort (teachers, governors and parents) and therefore there should be a common understanding of how the budget is being utilised.

(iv) Planning strategies involving the budget need to be flexible involving short- and long-term thinking and a willingness to accept a variety of approaches.

References

Davies, B. (1994) 'Managing resources' in Bush, T. and West-Burnham, J. *The Principles of Education Management* Longman.

Davies, B. and Ellison, L. (1990) *Managing the Primary School Budget* Northcote House.

Davies, B. and Ellison, L. (1992) *School Development Planning* Longman.

Handy, C. (1989) *The Age of Unreason* Arrow.

Skelton, M. Reeves, G. and Playfoot, D. (1991) *Development Planning for Primary Schools* Routledge.

8 Evaluation as an instrument in school development

Linda Ellison and Margaret Britton

Introduction

Earlier contributions to this book have pointed to the importance of evaluation — and to a tendency to neglect it! This chapter considers key ways of thinking about evaluation as part of a school's process of ongoing development. It then looks at how a case study primary school sought ways to examine its practice in this area with the aim of:

- describing the planning and implementation of a school-based evaluation process with a small group of teachers;
- establishing the implications for management of carrying out an evaluation for a whole school and considering how such evaluation might be managed to prepare for inspection while continuing to develop the school effectively.

The nature of evaluation

It is important to define 'evaluation' and the other terminology in this area in order to have a shared understanding. Three of the relevant terms and the connections between them are shown in Figure 8.1.

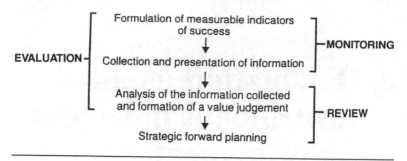

Figure 8.1   The evaluation process (Rogers and Badham 1992, p.4)

Rogers and Badham (1992, p.3) state that *monitoring* is '. . . the process of collecting and presenting information in relation to specific objectives on a systematic basis' while *review* is '. . . a considered reflection on progress using evaluation data to inform decisions for strategic planning.' *Evaluation* is the wider process which involves the systematic collection and analysis of information about the quality of provision and then the formation of value judgements (based on firm evidence) with a view to further action or development. The emphasis on 'further action' is significant because, if evaluation were to end at the point when a 'judgement of value' had been made, then this could lead to it being seen as a seal of approval — or disapproval. This would discourage teachers from becoming involved and make evaluation less useful in terms of the development of the school.

Evaluation should be an accepted part of the growth and development of the school. It is not a single, simple activity; it occurs in many forms, for several reasons and can be formal or informal. When a project is being planned, various questions should be asked about its evaluation:

- What is the purpose of the evaluation?
- What is to be evaluated?
- Who wants the evaluation?
- How will the evaluation be carried out?
  Who does it?
  When?
  By what method?
  Using what criteria?
- How will the evaluation report be used?

The purpose of evaluation

Evaluation is (or should be) primarily concerned with doing things better, both now and in the future. This developmental (or formative) function is to *improve* quality, for example to assist in the process of improving the effectiveness of meetings or of a curricular area. The process of evaluation allows for the identification of specific items for change so that the school can work on those to improve effectiveness.

In contrast to the developmental approach, there is the accountability or summative function of evaluation which is to *prove* quality. The formal, external evaluation such as is used by inspectors focuses on accountability. Here the purpose does not seem to be about developing the strengths of the school but of:

'. . . defining the outcomes of education and assessing their achievement by individual schools . . .' (Wilcox 1992, p.11).

This approach has relevance because professionals have been given resources and trusted to deliver effective education for pupils; they must demonstrate that they have fulfilled their responsibilities effectively and efficiently. In the case of the OFSTED process, the purpose seems to be to ensure that schools are efficient, economic and effective at a particular point in time.

However, this simple division of purpose into evaluation for development or for accountability does not reflect the true picture. An evaluation activity can be high or low as a developmental activity and high or low as a means of demonstrating accountability. If evaluation is to be useful and to make effective use of time, the information which is gathered should be suitable for both purposes. For example, the evaluation of a school's budget management could highlight areas where the process could allow for wider involvement in decision-making. At the same time, the evaluation could demonstrate the fairness of the resource distribution and that the correct procedures had been followed in terms of governor involvement. As another example, while development does not appear to be the main aim of the statistics on SATS results, a school can use the information to inform debate and further investigation in order to bring about improvements to the educational process.

The focus of the evaluation

The evaluation could have a very specific focus (for example, to find out how children with special educational needs are integrated within a particular class) or it could focus on a wide issue such

Table 8.1 Possible areas for evaluation

Area	Example of focus
pupils	pupil grouping
staff	effectiveness of teaching strategies
curriculum	coverage of the National Curriculum
teaching and learning materials	effectiveness of a mathematics scheme
school processes	planning, budgeting, home–school links
a specific project	encompassing several of the above, e.g. all aspects of the teaching and learning in physical education

as whole school development. Table 8.1 shows possible areas for evaluation.

In order to make the task more achievable, it is normally wise to limit the focus of the evaluation but, whatever the focus, the process should examine:

- goals;
- strategies and plans;
- actions;
- outcomes and impacts.

Evaluation can be carried out at different levels. For example, it may concern the work of an individual, a team (such as a year group or a Key Stage) or the whole school. There can also be evaluation of a wider nature, for example when a group of schools has participated in a particular project.

The audience for evaluation

Evaluation provides information for stakeholders, i.e. all those actually or potentially interested in what is being evaluated. This could be the staff, the governors, the parents, the LEA, the DfE or any body which has provided funding for a specific project. When planning an evaluation, it is therefore important to decide who the particular stakeholders are, what they need to know and what they will do with the information once it is made available to them. These factors determine the approach chosen and the way in which results will be presented and made available.

The evaluation approach

When planning the approach, decisions must be made concerning who is to carry out the evaluation (in terms of data gathering, co–ordination and reporting) and when, the process to be used and the criteria against which judgements will be made.

If staff are involved in evaluating themselves and their colleagues using an agreed set of criteria there will be a greater commitment to the outcomes than if outsiders evaluate the school using their own criteria. This internal evaluation may be informal or formal. As teachers, we constantly make judgements, albeit somewhat subjectively, about our own performance, the performance of colleagues and the performance of the school. What is needed is the formalisation of these processes so that they are an effective way of providing information to assist with school development. If judgements are gathered systematically they may help to identify problem areas and to suggest strategies for improvement. However, there are some dangers with internal evaluation: the focus may not be clearly defined; there may be too little planning; and the results may be rather subjective so that they are superficial or invalid.

This internal evaluation contrasts with the external approach, for example that which is carried out by advisers or consultants and which is of a formal nature. Examples of this would include OFSTED inspections or LEA inspections. In this more formal approach, the object of the evaluation is usually clearly defined, written and verbal information are systematically collected and conclusions drawn from the evaluation are usually well documented.

There are also some approaches which are not exclusively internal or external or which fall somewhere along the informal/formal continuum. An internal evaluation may involve staff in working with an external consultant. An internally devised evaluation could be of a formal nature, for example when colleagues systematically evaluate a curriculum development.

As LEAs now have very few resources to fund or to evaluate central projects and the OFSTED process will be a rare event, there is a greater need for schools to carry out their own internal or self-evaluations. This is also the form of evaluation most likely to succeed in a less than perfect climate as it puts the staff in control of the process. Many LEAs have produced and published guidelines for self-evaluation but they can be lengthy checklists which are value-laden and very daunting because they try to cover every aspect of school life. Leaders of self-evaluating organisations must become 'selective evaluators', i.e. they must determine a feasible focus and process.

There are various desirable characteristics which should be

considered when choosing who should carry out the evaluation. These would include: competency in research methodology and, depending on the nature of the evaluation, in data analysis; understanding of the school's context and of the object of the evaluation; the ability to relate appropriately to the individuals and groups involved.

When considering the timing of evaluation, either in the school year or in the lifecycle of a project, the emphasis should be on making evaluation manageable. Minor evaluations might be carried out termly or annually and major initiatives on a three or five year cycle. The timing and the cost of the time involved must be built in at the planning stage.

No single model could be used for all evaluation needs. The method of evaluation must be designed to fit the situation; it cannot simply be transferred from one school to another or, even within the same school, from the evaluation of one object or process to another. It is important to determine the type of information which is required before data are gathered so that it is then possible to decide on appropriate methods of data gathering. Evaluation can be carried out at a number of stages in the educational process. Osborne (1990, p.164) explains this in terms of a simple systems theory view of organisations.

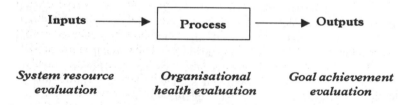

| *System resource evaluation* | *Organisational health evaluation* | *Goal achievement evaluation* |

A 'system resource' approach is a means of evaluating the relationship between the school and its environment and it takes the view that successful schools attract better or greater resources. Open enrolment, parental choice and the age-weighted pupil unit system of LMS add a great deal of meaning to this approach.

'Organisational health' evaluation is essentially a 'people-based' model which relies upon shared aims and a common understanding of those within the organisation. Its strengths lie in its holistic perspective to effectiveness and in its direct link with individual performance. This model's main problems are that efficiency may be confused with effectiveness and that it is so wide-ranging and judgemental.

In the 'goal achievement' approach, effectiveness is judged in terms of the extent to which objectives are met. Teachers are used to setting objectives, their achievement can be simply recorded and the process is readily understood. These factors make the method acceptable. The approach can be used to consider the extent to which national goals or ideals are being achieved or to measure whether the school's outputs are better than those of alternative systems. The validity of the process is dependent on the appropriateness of the goals and, because it is more concerned with 'product', it may not improve practice as it does not necessarily involve teacher development.

Whichever approach is chosen, a valid instrument needs to be developed. This should specify the information to be collected (limiting this to only that which is necessary), the source of the information and the means of recording. After it has been gathered, the evidence acquired during the evaluation process needs to be analysed against agreed criteria and interpreted.

Reporting on the evaluation

Reports should be concise and simple to understand so that staff still have the energy left to implement changes or developments highlighted by the evaluation. Consideration should be given to the way in which the report is presented to the audience. An oral presentation with accompanying documentation affords the opportunity to convey the desired meaning and to respond to questions. It is also important to decide how the report can best be used to achieve the original purposes of the evaluation process.

Summary

Evaluation uses the past to illuminate the future and is essential if a school is to gain the information for continuous improvement. Evaluation should be simple and should:

1. be included at the planning stage of any development;
2. involve a number of different viewpoints;
3. have clear purposes;
4. be accurate and methodologically sound;
5. involve a variety of methods of collecting good information;
6. be feasible, e.g. economic in its use of resources such as human, time, materials;
7. involve staff at all stages;
8. inform practice, for example professional development and curriculum development;

9. be legal and ethical;
10. be an ongoing rather than a periodic management function;
11. produce an account which is understood by its intended audiences.

SCHOOL CASE STUDY
Margaret Britton

A school based model for the project

As headteacher of a primary school, I wished to embark on a school-based project which would enable us to introduce a method of evaluating classroom processes. There were three main reasons for undertaking the project:

- to enable the management team to gather more detailed information about the development needs of the school so that we could improve the quality of teaching and learning;
- to look at how the evaluation of classroom practice could be managed so that the staff did not feel threatened and so that we could meet their development needs through the school development plan;
- to develop a more formalised approach to internal evaluation which should help the school to prepare for the formal external inspection laid out by the Office for Standards in Education (OFSTED).

One important way forward was to consider how to evaluate our teaching in order to identify strengths and weaknesses and to support the staff, for example, with further professional development. In this way, the inspection process would not be threatening or frightening because we would already be aware of some of our shortcomings and would be doing something about them. As we are to be 'evaluated' or 'inspected' as a profession we can help ourselves best by being clear about what we know works for us as individuals and for our pupils. The project had implications for a number of areas other than the management of evaluation. These were change management, human resource management (especially in relation to appraisal), time management and school development planning.

If the evaluation of classroom processes is to be introduced into a school, this requires changes in practice and expectation. If the change is to be managed effectively, then an appropriate approach needs to be selected. In this case, the model chosen used a sequence of developmental activities, shown in Figure 8.2.

This approach was chosen because it is clear and systematic, allowing for full staff involvement at all stages and also because past experience had shown that this flexible model worked in the school.

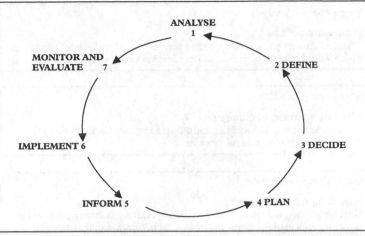

Figure 8.2   A project planning cycle (Day, Whitaker and Wren 1987, p.152)

Table 8.2   Managing change

Promote successful change	Hinder change management
The users have established the need for change.	The change is imposed.
Those who will use it have helped to create it. There is a shared understanding.	The plan is imposed. There is confusion and disparate understanding.
It does not threaten security or competency.	It makes teachers feel insecure and incompetent.
There have been previous successful changes.	It follows a series of failures.
The change is planned.	The change is unplanned.
The users will benefit from the change.	The users will not benefit or will be disadvantaged by the change.
The users value the change highly and are motivated by the extra work.	The users do not value the change and resent the extra work.
Time is planned for thorough implementation and there are resources available.	The process is rushed and there are inadequate resources.

Stage one — Analyse

Where are we now?
The headteacher to audit the current national, local and school situations
which would influence the evaluation of classroom practice

Stage two — Define

What do we want to change?
The headteacher to present the audit to teachers and consult them to
define the changes to current practice.

Stage three — Decide

Where do we want to go?
With colleagues, the headteacher to decide evaluation criteria, method of
gathering information, timescale, personnel involved, implementation,
monitoring, evaluation.

Stage four — Plan

How shall we get there?
Headteacher and pilot group of teachers to draw up and agree plans for
the introduction of evaluation.

Stage five — Inform

Who needs to know?
Communicate the plans to other colleagues.

Stage six — Implement

Let's try it!
Headteacher and pilot group.

Stage seven — Monitor and evaluate

How are we getting on?
Is it any good?
Where do we go from here?
Headteacher and pilot group of teachers to revise the evaluation method as
necessary.

Stage eight — Analyse (2)

Where are we now?
What have we learnt and what can we do with the information?
Whole staff to be involved.

Figure 8.3   A flowchart of the evaluation project

The effecting of change is a complex process which takes time. The plans should be sufficiently challenging to make them interesting but also sufficiently realistic and flexible to allow a measure of success over time. Table 8.2 shows factors which affect the change management process.

If the introduction of the evaluation of classroom practice was to be successful, then it was important to be aware of such factors. An outline plan for the project is shown in Figure 8.3. This was devised using the model in Figure 8.2 and bearing in mind the factors which would help to drive the successful introduction of a change. There then follows a more detailed analysis of the process as it occurred.

The application of a school–based model

Stage one

Analyse (June/July)

Where are we now?

The headteacher to audit the current national, local and school situations which would influence the evaluation of classroom practice.

It was important to be clear about the national and local contexts so that plans could take account of the situation in which the staff were working.

The key national factors which emerged at this stage were: the barrage of changes from central government; the emphasis on 'value for money', accountability and efficiency; the transfer of powers to schools under LMS; and the increases in responsibilities and roles of headteachers and governors. The reports on primary practice (see Chapter 1) provided a national forum for debate but had very little impact on the school. Staff were encouraged by the strengths identified in the reports and felt that the school could demonstrate many of these while the weaknesses were largely dismissed.

Against this background, there was a series of major changes within the local area. The school escaped the trauma of a large reorganisation during which time advisory support was focused mainly on the reorganising schools (although it was available in crisis situations). Reorganisation certainly seemed to lower morale throughout the area, particularly as it came alongside massive curriculum change. There were also uncertainties about the future school funding policies. The LEA's wish seemed to be to delegate as much as possible to the schools. A local commission made wide-ranging recommendations on school places, admission policies, formula funding and delegation and threw into doubt many established policies and procedures.

The school was a loser under formula funding so there had to be a variety of changes including the loss of two teaching posts. This resulted in larger classes and a loss of subject and age specific specialism. It was a very painful time for all those working in the school and added to the feeling of uncertainty. These events lowered morale, making teachers and support staff feel insecure and devalued. Large classes took their toll. Teachers were very tired and felt unable to do the best possible for the children. A developmental model of appraisal was about to be introduced but, despite reassurances, there was still a feeling amongst some that it was about weeding out the weak teachers. It was also emphasised that any development needs identified during the appraisal process would be used in planning the INSET programme and that everyone would get some help as a result. Appraisal was still viewed by all the staff without enthusiasm. Individual records of achievement and written reports to parents of all children had been issued for some time so the teachers did not view these as changes. The school did need to review its recording of the National Curriculum. Assessment was still a problem and much work needed to be done on agreement trials.

Staff had been involved in several regular evaluative activities. In the curricular areas, teachers had evaluated their teaching of history, geography, and science topics to inform further planning and teaching of the topic. An annual staff development interview based on self-evaluation had been carried out by me for several years and teachers had been encouraged to evaluate INSET courses which they had attended. Other 'one-off' evaluations had taken place after a number of activities. Teachers all evaluated the teaching and learning taking place in their classrooms on a daily basis, and used this information when planning for the next day. It was my intention to extend and regularise these self-evaluation activities within the school. The school had not had an HMI inspection for many years. A 'paired visit' from advisers had reported on the strengths and weaknesses of the school two years previous to this project. The staff were not (as the project commenced) familiar with the OFSTED inspection criteria.

In summary, the climate for the proposed project seemed inappropriate. However, in management terms, it was desirable in order to gain deeper insights into the quality of teaching in the school. Needs were to be identified and supported through

Table 8.3   A force field analysis of the proposed project

Drivers	Restrainers
1. The users recognise the need for the evaluation of teaching.	1. Inspection is to be imposed but, in terms of the school's developmental stage, the time is not right.
2. Those who will use the evaluation have helped to establish the criteria.	2. It could well be confused with observations carried out as part of appraisal and therefore seen as threatening.
3. It does not threaten security or competency as it is carried out by the headteacher.	3. The users may have difficulty in seeing the benefits of preparing for inspection as other innovations (e.g. National Curriculum) have been subject to massive change.
4. The users will, in the long term, benefit from the change.	
5. There have been previous successful changes implemented in the school.	4. The change has to share available time and resources with other externally imposed innovations.
6. Financial resources can be made available.	
7. The innovation is planned.	

the development plan so that the school could begin to prepare for inspection. The context for the project is shown in the force-field analysis in Table 8.3.

Stage two

Define (September/October)

What do we want to change?

The headteacher to present the audit to teachers and consult them to define the changes to current practice.

In order to involve all the teaching staff, a staff meeting was arranged to open up the debate on classroom practice and to explain the proposed evaluation project. It was structured in various sections which are described below.

1. Introduction

I explained my wish to promote a positive attitude to evaluation and stressed throughout that evaluation is about spotting the actions that breed success, not about looking for faults. Through effective evaluation the teacher can recognise success and can use it to adjust future plans.

2. Survey

Each member of staff was asked to write down responses to the question, 'What in your opinion constitutes good practice for this school in the current educational climate?' (e.g. classroom organisation, discipline, knowledge of how children learn, teaching strategies). The teachers did not collaborate. Most seemed to find it difficult to make general statements about 'good practice' and were very much thinking in terms of their own specific situation in the school. Many of the comments appeared to be negative, such as the problems with meeting National Curriculum requirements or the impossibility of large classes. The teachers' responses were grouped and are shown in Figure 8.4.

3. Reading

The staff were given selected texts on classroom practice and this prompted more positive comments. The passages seemed to help the teachers to focus on the question a little more.

4. Group discussion

The teachers elected to group by Key Stage taught as they felt that there would be more common ground. The KS1 group seemed to have produced a great deal of agreement about 'good practice' and the discussion was lively. The teachers were able to make many *general* comments about what constituted 'good practice'. Members of the KS2 group were quite negative in their approach and spent a lot of time debating the difficulties of having a large class such as the constraints that this put upon curriculum content, match and teaching strategies. This group was much less able to agree on what constitutes 'good practice'. They listed 14 criteria and had more to add.

Both groups had written their criteria for 'good practice' on large sheets of paper. These were presented in a feedback session. The lists were pinned up and we looked for common strands. The discussion was interesting and teachers were pleased to see that there were, in fact, similarities in their lists, although fewer than I had hoped. The ones identified were:

- discipline;
- relationships with children;

		CRITERIA FOR 'GOOD PRACTICE'
C U R R I C U L U M		'Work matched to ability. Children achieve success.' Match. Clear aims and purposes. 'Children must be well motivated.' Use first hand experience. Assess/record and evaluate to inform planning. Continuity within school, age group, class. Meet National Curriculum requirements.
R E S O U R C E S	H U M A N & M A T E R I A L	Well organised and appropriate resources. Children are clear about classroom organisation. Good relationships with children. Maintain discipline. Good relationships with adults (colleagues and parents). Catering for social and emotional development.
T E A C H I N G		Use flexible teaching strategies ('fitness for purpose') Spend time teaching/instructing. Promote positive attitudes - a good ethos. Teachers share expertise and talents. Class size.

Figure 8.4   Criteria for good classroom practice

- match of work to ability;
- the organisation of classroom resources;
- the use of assessment.

Staff were asked to try to consider how they would recognise 'good practice' in a classroom. Most had great difficulty in thinking about this in general terms and kept returning to their own situation in which they felt handicapped by large classes and an overloaded and complex curriculum. The lack of opportunities to see colleagues at work meant that they did not feel able to answer the questions fully. The majority at some point in the discussion expressed a feeling of inadequacy and said that they felt uncertain about what was expected of teachers. The need for consistency of approach to curricular, organisational and disciplinary matters was stressed on a number of occasions. Staff seemed to recognise the need for a 'whole school approach' yet it was interesting to see how, in their written responses, there seemed to be a great variance in what they considered important. Consensus is notoriously difficult to achieve amongst a group of staff.

In discussion the shared criteria were agreed and prioritised. The 'flexible use of teaching strategies' was added to the list. The list of possible criteria established by the end of the discussion is shown in Figure 8.5.

---

1. Relationships/Ethos

   To include discipline. Phrases used were 'firm, fair, consistent' and 'positive, warm, caring, motivating.'

---

2. Flexible teaching strategies

   Range of strategies
   Appropriate to task
   Appropriate to class size
   Appropriate to space available

---

3. Classroom Organisation

   Materials
   Children
   Other adults (classroom assistants, special needs assistants, parents)

---

4. Planning for match

   Clear aims
   National curriculum requirements
   Differentiated tasks
   Challenging for varied abilities
   Success achieved and recognised

---

5. Assessment of learning outcome

   Fair, consistent, honest, regular feedback

Figure 8.5 Suggested criteria for the evaluation of classroom practice

The remaining discussion questions (to do with the *process* of evaluation) were not dealt with as time was running out and it would be more helpful to return to these when criteria were more focused.

5. What next?

I needed the continued interest and support of at least a small group of staff so it was important to reach some agreement before closing the meeting. The staff were asked if they would be willing to try self-evaluation or to be evaluated against the criteria by me as the headteacher. Everyone said that they would be happy to be evaluated by me but no one wanted to evaluate their own work. The lessons learned from this meeting were that:

- teachers found difficulty in thinking about this issue in broad generic terms;
- teachers did not mention planning as a criterion for good teaching although they all plan thoroughly for their own teaching;
- the staff were not as far on in their thinking about 'good practice' as expected.

Stage three

Decide (October)

Where do we want to go?

With colleagues, the headteacher to decide evaluation criteria, method of gathering information, timescale, personnel involved, implementation, monitoring, evaluation.

Three teachers volunteered to help with this stage. Using the proposed criteria for evaluation agreed during the staff meeting, I then looked at a range of materials available for self-evaluation and for whole school evaluation. Many seemed to be merely checklists and there was nothing which seemed appropriate for our purpose. The most useful guidance came from Hopkins who views evaluation as an important tool in school development and defines it as a form of classroom research which is:

> an act undertaken by teachers either to improve their own or a colleague's teaching theory in practice. Classroom research generates hypotheses about teaching from the experience of

teaching, and encourages teachers to use this research to make their teaching more effective' (Hopkins 1989, p.98).

This seemed to be in line with my thinking. He goes on to suggest a grid for 'developmental performance indicators' which is shown in Figure 8.6.

Headings, Issue or Theme	Performance Indicators		Antici-pated Outcome	Action by whom	Deadlines	Starting point	LEA or school priority
	Key Compo-nents	Subdivision of key compo-nents					

Figure 8.6   **Developmental performance indicators (Hopkins 1989, p.105)**

This was adapted to arrive at a draft evaluation schedule (for the final version see Figure 8.7) based on the criteria generated by the teachers at the staff meeting. The draft was taken to a meeting with the three volunteer teachers. They were interested to see how 'their' criteria had been developed and were now presented in a grid form. A great deal of discussion centred around what was understood by the terms used such as 'exploratory style'. Some of my initial proposals for criteria under each key component were then expanded or changed.

The group felt that it would be helpful to have an agreed way of recording observations and some way of summarising these which did not involve a great deal of writing. A system of grading was agreed as follows:

(a)   indicates a strength (individual teacher);
A   indicates a strength (school);
(b)   indicates a satisfactory level (individual teacher);
B   indicates a satisfactory level (school);
(c)   indicates a weakness (individual teacher);
C   indicates a weakness (school);
*   teacher requests help;
**   teacher indicates a whole school need;
√   individual need identified by evaluator/observer;
√√   school need identified by evaluator/observer.

Name_____   Year Group taught_____   Date of Observations 1 _____

                                                                         2 _____

                                                                         3 _____

THEME	PERFORMANCE INDICATORS	CRITERIA	EVIDENCE
			Method
1. Teacher's relationship with children	There are warm, open relationships		Observation
	Key components:		
	• mutual respect	• good manners, good listening (teacher and children)	
	• establishes a quiet working atmosphere when required	• there is quiet working atmosphere when required	
	• sympathetic understanding of individual needs	• flexible $\left\{\begin{array}{l}\text{response}\\\text{approach to}\end{array}\right.$ individual need	
	• uses praise	• praises children appropriately	
	• elicits and controls children's responses	• uses questioning appropriately	
	• shows clearly what is expected of the children	• clear targets set for children	
	• not sarcastic	• responses do not use sarcasm	
	• maintains firm, fair expectations for behaviour	• clear, consistent classroom rules	
	• uses humour appropriately	• humour is used appropriately	
	• involved with children outside the classroom	• relationship extends beyond formal teaching sessions	

COMMENTARY

RECOMMENDATIONS

Figure 8.7   The final evaluation grids

Name_____   Year Group taught_____ Date of Observations 1 _____
                                                                         2 _____
                                                                         3 _____

THEME	PERFORMANCE INDICATORS	CRITERIA	EVIDENCE
2. Teaching Strategies	Use of a range of teaching styles and strategies	Teacher demonstrates the use of a variety of styles as listed	Method Observation Teacher's Planning file
	Key components:		
	• uses didactic style appropriately		
	• uses exploratory style appropriately		
	• uses whole class teaching appropriately		
	• uses group teaching appropriately		
	• uses individual teaching appropriately		
	• uses flexible groupings as appropriate		
	• uses team teaching appropriately		
	• uses unqualified support appropriately		
	• recognises the strengths and weakness of the above	Is able to give reasons for selecting a particular approach/approaches	
			Interview

COMMENTARY

RECOMMENDATIONS

Figure 8.7   Continued

Name_____   Year Group taught_____   Date of Observations   1 _____

2 _____

3 _____

THEME	PERFORMANCE INDICATORS	CRITERIA	EVIDENCE
3. Organisation of Resources	The physical arrangement of furniture and resources supports the teaching and learning Key components: • the furniture is arranged to support classroom organisation and teaching style • resources are stored appropriately • resources are accessible • the equipment is cared for • other areas of school are used when appropriate	 • arrangement of furniture is appropriate for the age group and the activity • resources are stored safely • children can collect resources when needed • the equipment is in good, clean condition and there is evidence of care (e.g. counting items, cleaning etc.) • groups/individuals working in other areas of the school	Method Observation

COMMENTARY

RECOMMENDATIONS

Figure 8.7   Continued

Name_____   Year Group taught_____   Date of Observations 1 _____

                                                                    2 _____

                                                                    3 _____

THEME	PERFORMANCE INDICATORS	CRITERIA	EVIDENCE
4. Match	The work is well matched to each child's stage of development		
	Key components:		
	• the needs of the children are assessed individually	• written and aural evidence of teacher's assessment	Individual pupil records Interview
	• the teaching is planned to cater for the needs of individual children	• teacher's planning caters for different needs, indicating individual/group programmes	Teacher's Planning file Talk to children
	• the learning experiences selected are appropriate	• children are challenged by the experience and achieve success	Observation Children's work
	• the resource material is matched to the learning situation	• any worksheet/card etc. to support the teaching and learning	Observation Resources used
	• if groups are used, then the children are grouped according to need	• groupings are flexible and respond to need	Teacher's Planning file

COMMENTARY

RECOMMENDATIONS

Figure 8.7   Continued

Name_____   Year Group taught_____ Date of Observations 1 _____

2 _____

3 _____

THEME	PERFORMANCE INDICATORS	CRITERIA	EVIDENCE
5. Planning	A clear understanding of objectives for the class in relationship to National Curriculum and the aims of the school policy	* An agreed school policy to be in place first	Method School policies
	Key components:		
	• continuity and progression across the curriculum	• good relationships with colleagues	Method Observation Teacher's Planning file Interview
		• shared planning	
		• refers to school policy and NC when planning	
		• half term plans	
		• weekly plans	
		• daily plans	
		• evaluation of the plans (formative and summative)	
		• aware of what is happening in other classes	

COMMENTARY

RECOMMENDATIONS

Figure 8.7   Continued

Name_____   Year Group taught_____   Date of Observations   1 _____

                                                                          2 _____

                                                                          3 _____

THEME	PERFORMANCE INDICATORS	CRITERIA	EVIDENCE
6. Assessing and recording individual progress	Clear, consistent criteria are used in assessing children's learning	* There should be an agreed school policy	
	Key components:		Method
	• assessments are systematically recorded	• assessments are made • records are made	Individual Pupil records
	• these assessments are used to inform the teacher's planning	• evidence in planning to match individual need	Teacher's Planning file
	• records of academic and personal achievements are kept	• records of achievement are regularly up-dated	
	• the records are passed on to the next class/school	• records are cumulative	

COMMENTARY

RECOMMENDATIONS

Figure 8.7   Continued

Name_____   Year Group taught_____   Date of Observations   1 _____

                                                                 2 _____

                                                                  3 _____

THEME	PERFORMANCE INDICATORS	CRITERIA	EVIDENCE
			Method
7. Self-evaluation of teaching and learning	Formative and summative evaluation informs the plans for teaching and learning		Teachers's Planning file
			Written Evaluation
	Key components:		
	• daily evaluation of teaching and learning	• use evaluation to inform next day's planning	
	• weekly/fortnightly evaluation of teaching and learning	• use evaluation to monitor progress and revise half term plans	
	• half termly evaluation of teaching and learning (topic)	• summative evaluation of teaching and learning (topic)	
	• evaluation across the curriculum at the end of the term	• summative evaluation of teaching and learning for the term to be used as a basis for next term's plans	
	• evaluation across the curriculum at the end of the year	• summative evaluation of the year's teaching and learning used to inform subsequent plans for teaching and learning	

COMMENTARY

RECOMMENDATIONS

Figure 8.7   Continued

It was also agreed that information about teaching qualities should be collected from other sources such as interviews and planning notes, rather than just from classroom observations. Much of the discussion focused on how the evaluation might be carried out, given the pressure on time. It was felt that it would be better if more than one person carried out an evaluation as this would possibly be less subjective and that observations should be carried out on more than one occasion. Then it was mentioned that the curriculum area being taught at the time might alter what was seen. Not everyone agreed: it was pointed out that many skills of teaching are the same whatever the subject and that only the subject knowledge/expertise would be different. Eventually the group agreed that the point of *this* evaluation was to look at generic teaching qualities.

The group was happy for me to amend the proposed grid and to carry out some observations of their teaching with an early opportunity for feedback if required. No one else wanted to be involved in carrying out an evaluation at this stage.

Stage four

Plan (November)

How shall we get there?

Headteacher and pilot group of teachers to draw up and agree plans for the introduction of evaluation.

A further short meeting was called for the volunteer pilot group. At this I presented the amended observation grid and no further amendments were suggested. All the teachers felt that it would be better to start observations in the Spring term as the lead-up to Christmas can be hectic and not always as planned.

Stage five

Inform (December)

Who needs to know?

Communicate the plans to other colleagues.

As part of a staff meeting, I showed the evaluation grids and told everyone what the pilot group had agreed. The teachers showed a polite interest but asked no questions. Perhaps they hoped they would not have to be involved and that, if they kept quiet, the problem would go away!

Stage six

Implement (January/February)

Let's try it!

Headteacher and pilot group.

Classroom observation

The times for the observations were negotiated on a daily basis to fit into the busy and sometimes unpredictable schedule of a headteacher. Very quickly, it was realised that the original evaluation grid had shortcomings and revisions were needed. Grades could not be given immediately so some cumulative form of recording observations and then grading later was needed. Each time I noticed that a criterion had been met, it was recorded with a tick. The same form was to be used for each of the three observations so that a cumulative record could be kept. There was too much to consider if all seven themes were used on the same occasion but the evaluation themes could be divided into two groups. Group A needed to be evaluated during teaching while Group B could be evaluated from documentation and interview.

Group A
Theme 1   Teacher's relationship with children
Theme 2   Teacher's strategies
Theme 3   Organisation of resources
Theme 4   Match
Group B
Theme 5   Planning
Theme 6   Assessing and recording individual progress
Theme 7   Self-evaluation of teaching and learning

This reduced the workload during observation. Interviews would need to be arranged and documentation collected in order to evaluate the Group B themes and some items on Group A themes, particularly Match. Other small changes were made to the original grid in order to make it more manageable and useful. Theme 4 (Match) needed other changes because the methods of collecting evidence were so varied.

Further observations were delayed until these changes had been effected. The remaining observations were carried out using the revised format which proved to be more helpful. There was still a problem with grading teaching quality as the three categories used (see page 132) were rather broad and some 'fine-tuning' was required. It was thought that the evaluation schedule would become more helpful as other observers used it, found difficulties and re-designed it. It should be a document which is responsive to the needs of the school and should, therefore evolve over time.

Planning files

I was used to reading planning files regularly so this part of the evaluation seemed relatively straightforward. It was helpful that the school also had a policy for planning because certain criteria were met as they were already a part of the usual planning process, especially for theme 7 (Evaluation of teaching and learning) and theme 5 (Planning). The elements in theme 4 (Match) which required me to look for evidence in the planning file were also satisfied because differentiation of tasks and indications of groupings were already part of the school's planning policy. It was decided that, although it would be interesting and informative to look at planning and evaluation in general, it would also be important to look in detail at the planning and evaluation of the sessions observed. Any questions arising from this would be dealt with during the interview session.

Pupil records and pupil 'interviews'

Although the school has a policy for record keeping, they were not always up-to-date. Written records were not obviously being used to inform planning. Teachers seemed to be making more use of daily evaluations of teaching and learning in their planning than they were of the individual records. This was an area which would need to be questioned in the interview sessions.

Pupil 'interviews' were used to establish whether the pupils understood the task which they were asked to do and whether they

found it interesting and challenging. The questions asked were of
the type:

*'Can you explain to me what you are doing? Is it difficult for
you? What is interesting about it? Is . . . (the teacher) going to
be pleased with you when you have done it? (i.e. are you likely
to be successful?)*

Where there was clarity and match in the teacher's planning,
the pupils were able to respond well to these questions.

Pupils' written work

Where children produced some written work in the session
observed, I collected some examples from across the ability range.
These were looked at alongside the teacher's planning and children's
individual records. In the main, the work produced fulfilled the
teacher's aims to a satisfactory or better level. Because the individual
pupil records were not up to date, it was difficult to tell how far the
work was representative of the child. It was becoming clear that the
school might need to look at its individual record keeping system.
As headteacher, I knew that this was not a problem peculiar to the
pilot group and was indeed a whole school issue.

Interviews

I interviewed each of the three teachers in the pilot group for about
30 minutes. The teachers had prior notice of the questions which
were:
1. Theme 2 — Teaching strategies
    When I was in your classroom you were using . . . style
    of teaching. What was your reason for using that particular
    approach at that time?
2. Theme 4 and theme 6 — Match and Individual pupil records
    Can you explain to me how you assess children's achievements
    and needs? Do you record these assessments and what use do
    you make of the records when planning?
3. Theme 5 — Planning
    How do you find out what is happening in other classes?
    Is continuity important? How far does the school achieve
    continuity?

Teachers were all quite clear about their use of various teaching
strategies, saying that they chose the approach most suitable for the
occasion — 'fitness for purpose'. All said that larger classes meant
that there was less time to spend with individuals and that they

were making more use of whole class and group teaching when appropriate in order to create more opportunities to work with individuals. Two teachers who had special needs assistants working in their classrooms also pointed out that this help, used wisely and planned for, was helpful to more than just the child with special educational needs.

Assessment and recording of achievement seemed to be presenting quite a problem. This had been suggested by the written evidence which I had seen and was confirmed by the pilot group. The problem identified by all three teachers was the difficulty of assessing against the National Curriculum statements of attainment. The number of assessments required for each child and the number of children in the classes made this a huge task. One teacher suggested that perhaps, as we became increasingly familiar with the National Curriculum, the task would seem easier.

All said that they did not record children's achievements on a daily or weekly basis but did try to update the records at the end of the term. They found the daily evaluation of teaching and learning which they carry out as part of their planning a more useful tool. They acknowledged that records are important but felt that time spent on planning for effective teaching was more productive than 'filling in little boxes'.

All three stressed that continuity is important but that it is difficult to experience what is happening in other classes. They stated that to be involved in shared planning is helpful, but that it would be good to have the experience of working alongside colleagues to see how they 'bring the plans to life' in the classrooms. None of them seemed sure about curriculum continuity throughout the school but felt that, because teachers passed on written records to the child's next class, then there was some continuity. They were less sure about continuity in terms of behaviour, effort, and expectations.

Stage seven

Monitor and evaluate(January/February/March)

How are we getting on?

Is it any good?
Where do we go from here?
Headteacher and pilot group of teachers to revise the evaluation method as necessary.

This activity had been taking place to some extent throu
the implementation stage but it was now necessary to d
more formally. The first stage was to feedback the results o
evaluations to the pilot group and to obtain their reactions to
process.

In the feedback sessions to individual teachers each one
shown the evaluation records. It was generally agreed that apprai
should identify individual development needs but that this form
evaluation would, by taking a less focused look, identify oth
important areas and would be a valuable and useful process. On
teacher suggested that the evaluation schedule could be used in th
classroom observations during the appraisal process. The teachers
had not found the 'observation' part of the evaluation particularly
threatening but had been more wary of the interview. All said
they had felt happy to talk about their teaching strategies but had
felt uncertain about the assessment and recording question. One
suggested that if we were to run some agreement trials we might find
them helpful, both for assessing children's work and for fostering
some continuity in teacher expectations. The teachers felt very
encouraged that individual strengths had been recognised through
the evaluation. They were pleased that areas for development had
also been recognised but wondered where the resources would come
from to allow a development programme to take place.

It was interesting to see how the criteria for evaluation of
teaching processes devised by the school compared with those
planned for the OFSTED process. Figure 8.8 shows the comparison.
There are no OFSTED criteria which are not met by the
school's themes but themes 3 and 7 are not covered under
OFSTED's *Quality of Teaching — Guidance* (HMCI 1992, p.21).
OFSTED uses much clearer criteria for grading teaching quality.
The inspection team uses a six-point scale. Three areas are graded in
the observation of any lesson: the 'quality of teaching'; the 'quality
of learning'; and the 'standards of achievement displayed in lesson.'
These grades are then aggregated to give an 'overall grade'. The six
point scale gives greater flexibility than my three point scale. Before
using the evaluation schedules again in the school we changed to
those to be used by inspection teams. Alterations were made to
the statement for grade three to make it clear that 'satisfactory'
should not be taken as meaning 'mediocre'. These grades were
much easier to use as they were more specific. The three grades
used to indicate a school need or strength were retained, but the
definitions were made more specific. As 'ticks' were now being used
to record observations of evidence, the symbols used for recording
a school need were changed from a tick or double tick to 'N' and
'NN'. A few further observations were then carried out and the

School Performance Indicators		OFSTED Criteria
Theme 1	There are warm, open realtionships.	'Relationships are positive and promote pupils' motivation'.
Theme 2	Use of a range of teaching styles and strategies.	'The teaching methods suit the topic or subject as well as the pupils;'
Theme 3	The physical arrangement of furniture and resources supports the teaching and learning.	
Theme 4	The work is well matched to each child's stage of development.	'. . . pupils acquire knowledge, skills and understanding progressively and at a good pace' 'They' (the lessons) 'cater appropriately for the learning of pupils of differing abilities and interests, and ensure the full participation of all' '. . . the conduct of the lesson signals high expectations of all pupils and sets high but attainable challenges.'
Theme 5	A clear understanding of objectives for the class in relationship to National Curriculum and the aims of the school policy.	'The lessons have clear aims and purposes. National Curriculum Attainment Targets and programmes of study are taken fully into account'
Theme 6	Clear consistent criteria are used in assessing children's learning.	'There is regular feedback which helps pupils to make progress, both through thoughtful marking and discussion of work with pupils'
Theme 7	Formative and summative evaluation informs the plans for teaching and learning.	

Figure 8.8 The school evaluation criteria and the OFSTED criteria

revised schedule was found to be easier to use and the gradings more meaningful.

Stage eight

Analyse (2) (March)

Where are we now?

What have we learnt and what can we do with the information? Whole staff to be involved.

The stages described so far formed only the first cycle of a project. I had the opportunity to trial an evaluation process with a small group of teachers and, by doing this, learned more about the school. The next step would be to involve the whole staff in hearing about the evaluation from the pilot group and then, as a group to begin to analyse the current situation and to start the planning of the next cycle.

As a result of carrying out the evaluation, the school has an agreed set of criteria against which the quality of teaching can be judged. These criteria match, very closely, those of OFSTED. Some teachers have experienced the evaluation process and have been involved in its development. Teachers were involved from the beginning and felt a sense of ownership of the criteria and therefore they valued judgements made of their teaching using their criteria. Although only a small group was involved in the actual evaluation, valuable lessons were learned about carrying out the evaluations and about the methods of collecting information. All the teachers have, to some extent, been made aware of the nature of evaluation of the teaching process. Some individual and school needs have been identified and some strengths have been recognised.

Management implications

The evaluation process was a learning experience for me as head-teacher and also for the school as a whole. We learned:
1. that it is better to be specific when writing criteria and in describing grades;
2. something of the detail of the teaching processes currently in use in the school;
3. that pilot schemes are needed so that processes can be refined before full scale implementation;

4. that it is sometimes necessary to be proactive in bringing about change, even when the time does not seem ideal. The headteacher should be in a good position to see the development needs of the school in relation to the national and local context. Although it is desirable to allow the focus for change to be generated by the whole staff, there is a risk that the urgent will cloud the need to do the important;

5. time is always at a premium and must be used effectively. Evaluation should not be seen as an end in itself but should be seen to inform future developments;

6. that evaluation of the evaluation process (meta-evaluation) is important. For example it was found that it is possible to carry out the process (especially observation) over a shorter period of time if one is familiar with the school;

7. that the change management framework adopted for this project (see Figure 8.2) was, once again, helpful. It is often reassuring to staff if the same process is used for managing a variety of initiatives.

The information gathered by managing the evaluation process could be used in several ways. Individual teacher needs identified in the evaluations could be used alongside the needs identified in appraisal when planning that teacher's development programme. The observations schedule could be used:

- as a checklist for self-evaluation, either as a regular activity or as part of the appraisal process;
- for the evaluation of a colleague's teaching (perhaps as part of appraisal);
- for the headteacher to evaluate all teachers;
- as a useful starting point when developing evaluation criteria for other school activities.

The management strategies learned in carrying out this project could be applied to other management situations. For example, the process could be extended to look at factors which promote a successful learning environment. The knowledge and skills learnt will be useful in managing the school's preparation for inspection. Although it would not be possible or sensible to look at every area of the curriculum at once, it would be useful to focus on one curricular area in order to identify development needs. The area chosen would then be the main curriculum development focus for the next SDP. In this way, whole school needs could be identified and a programme could be planned and resourced to improve the teaching of that subject throughout the school. The evaluation criteria could be a key section of school policy. Because the generic skills of teaching and learning are present in every subject, then these would also be regularly under review and staff development could be planned to develop those skills.

Conclusion

Evaluation implies potential change. It will throw many previously held values into question and may challenge beliefs. The climate within the organisation must be ready to deal with these uncertainties or evaluation may become a threat which unsettles staff and establishes doubts about the effectiveness of the school. There are enormous change management implications here. Evaluation is often viewed with suspicion as it is bound up with ideas of accountability. Teachers need to be clear about why the evaluation is taking place, its purpose, who it is for and whose values are to be used. If the evaluation is seen in a negative way then its conclusions are unlikely to be acted upon. If the climate is right and the approach is sensitive, then the evaluation process helps to clarify strengths and weaknesses by establishing facts and removing doubt and uncertainty. Greater clarity can help in policy formation and overall school development. Staff are also being helped to see how issues highlighted in the evaluation process can result in further training and professional development for them and a change in resourcing for the school.

References

Day, C., Whitaker, P. and Wren, D. (1987) *Appraisal and Professional Development in Primary Schools* Open University Press.

Hopkins, D. (1989) *Evaluation for School Development* Oxford University Press.

HMCI (1992) *Handbook for the Inspection of Schools* Office for Standards in Education.

Osborne, A. 1990 'Managing the evaluation of schools' in Davies, B. *et al.* (eds) *Education Management for the 1990s* Longman.

Rogers, G. and Badham, L. (1992) *Evaluation in Schools* Routledge.

Wilcox, B. (1992) *Time-constrained evaluation* Routledge.

9 Meeting the management challenge of the future

Brent Davies

> If it ain't broke don't fix it! *or* if it ain't broke you haven't
> looked hard enough?

While this book has focused on ways of thinking about managing
today's reality it is necessary that we develop not only the management skills to operate in today's educational environment but also
the educational leadership capacity to challenge today's orthodoxy
and to envision what the future educational and societal framework
will be. It is one of the roles of leaders of educational organisations
to interpret and make sense of future realities for members of their
organisations. A child starting school at the age of five in September
1994 and going on to higher education will not complete his/her
education until the year 2010 at the earliest! What is more, that
child could be working with technologies that have not yet been
invented in an organisation that has yet to be created! Beare and
Slaughter (1993, p.145) use the concept of the extended present in
Figure 9.1. This illustrates that we need to have not only a view of
our current situation but also of the longer-term future if we are to
set our management actions in the appropriate context.

The problem that faces the educational leader in the primary
school is that incremental patterns of management behaviour and
patterns of thinking predominate. One of the means of adjusting

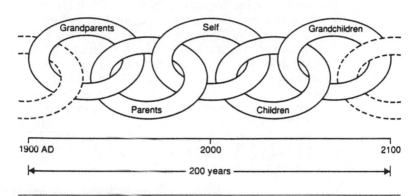

Figure 9.1   The extended present — the family chain

to new ways of thinking is to adopt ideas from the total quality management movement. Certainly, concepts of focusing on the customer, setting benchmarks, defining fitness for purpose and continuous improvement are valuable ways of thinking in establishing effective management for the year 2000 and beyond. These four ideas can be seen to be working themselves through certain parts of the education system. There is now a greater focus on the customer, for example by listening and taking into account the views of parents and children, both in the formal mechanisms of school choice and in the approaches to management within the school. Setting up benchmarks and defining fitness for purpose have taken a significant step forward during the first half of the 1990s. The National Curriculum and standardised assessment tasks (SATs) have put a floor under standards which have established a framework within which inspection through OFSTED has been able to assess progress. While it must be accepted that OFSTED is a quality control mechanism allied to the benchmarking features of the National Curriculum and SATs, its requirement for schools to produce action plans does develop an improvement culture. The development of an improvement culture is also evident with the increased emphasis on school development planning as a means of school improvement but, as Davies (1994) points out, incremental improvement, while beneficial, may not be enough to cope with the changes facing schools in the future. These quality approaches may be the absolute minimum preconditions for a school to be operating in ten years time. What is probably needed is a more radical and fundamental rethink of the nature of society, education and the role of the school.

One of the ways of achieving this fundamental re-thinking is to adopt the concepts embedded in the reengineering movement. Reengineering, as defined by Hammer and Champy (1993, p.32), involves 'the *fundamental rethinking* and *radical redesign* of *business processes* to achieve *dramatic* improvement in critical contemporary measures of performance, such as cost, quality, service and speed'.

Why should this be necessary? Can't successful organisations carry on as before and continue to be successful? Hammer and Champy suggest that three forces are driving companies into a new and unfamiliar operational context. Those forces are *Customers*, *Competition*, and *Change*. This chapter now looks at each of these in broad economic terms and then explores the educational parallels.

Customers

The mass market developed in the 1950s, 1960s and 1970s. During this time customers were glad to receive any product but this situation has now broken down into a 'quality product' approach aimed at individual customers. Hammer and Champy (1993, p.18) express this as 'Customers — consumers and corporations alike — demand products and services designed for their unique and particular needs. There is no longer any such notion as *the* customer; there is only *this* customer, the one with whom a seller is dealing at the moment and who now has the capacity to indulge his or her own personal tastes. The mass market has broken into pieces, some as small as a single customer'. The following key factors can be seen as emerging:

- customers have experienced quality and good service and expect more and better quality in the future;
- customers are better informed, have more data such as consumer reports on which to make their decisions and they know their legal rights in cases of dispute;
- customers are less deferential;
- customers dictate what they want, when they want it and how they want to pay for it;
- customers want to be seen as individuals and to receive a customised product;
- customers are aware that there is plentiful supply and that they can pick and choose;
- if you lose *this* customer, there is no guarantee of a replacement.

This shift in power towards the consumer is having a profound effect in the business world. Management emphasis on total quality management, customer care and niche marketing can all be seen as attempts to focus on individual customer needs and to provide the quality of individualised service needed to stay in business.

The parallel trends in the education sector in general and the school sector in particular are almost identical. National Curriculum and the publication of GCSE and SATs results are providing benchmarks to help parents to measure the quality of education received and the achievement made by their children. The culture in which the school knew best and parents were kept at arm's length has been replaced by a move to a more equal home/school relationship. Selection of school through open enrolment legislation has increased choice and given more power to the parent as customer.

Competition

> Good performers drive out the inferior, because the lowest price, the highest quality, the best service available from any one of them soon becomes the standard for all competitors. Adequate is no longer good enough. If a company can't stand shoulder to shoulder with the world's best in a competitive category, it soon has no place to stand at all (Hammer and Champy 1993, p.21).

What are the features of the intensified competition that is sweeping through companies and forcing them to reassess their position? The following highlight some of these:

- The nature of the competition is increasingly global. Low wage economies of the Far East and China are allying themselves to high technology to threaten Western firms and there are more recent forms of competition from Eastern Europe and the old Soviet Empire.
- Technological leaders are emerging with new firms starting up without the 'baggage' that traditional firms have in terms of structures and costs and they are driving the traditional firms out of business.
- Niche targeting of specific markets means that entrepreneurial firms are establishing bridgeheads in markets previously dominated by large corporations.
- marketing the same product by different criteria to fit different market circumstances is increasingly evident.

Does any of this apply to education? Isn't education somehow different from the business world? While it may be different, education is not isolated from the pressures and trends that are making themselves increasingly evident. Global competition has

a profound impact on the future of our children. Unless they
develop high quality thinking, problem-solving and technological
skills to compete with the best in the world, they will be competing
for the low wage/low skill jobs! How do our children compare
internationally on maths and scientific scores? The results to date
are not very encouraging.

Technological leaders are emerging not only in industry but also
in education. In the United States, Hughes Aircraft Corporation
has launched a multi-million dollar satellite system focused on
the education market. Its 'Galaxy' project is linking two hundred
schools across America. The Whittle Corporation in America is
setting up 250 schools which are heavily technology-based and
which will compete directly with local schools. Parents in rural
areas of Canada are setting up their own schools using satellite
educational channels in preference to sending their children to state
schools. Why put up with a poor maths co-ordinator when, for the
same money, you can subscribe to the best maths channel in the
world? The technology of teaching has not changed for hundreds of
years with the dominant approach being a teacher, a book and pupils
in a room. Teachers are the largest cost on a budget and a significant
public sector budget deficit makes the possibility of large sums of
extra finance a remote possibility. The use of alternative teaching
technologies in the future may be the only way to secure significant
increases in learning outcomes. Is the future going to encompass
larger groups of children with one fully qualified teacher working
with para-professional help in an environment rich in computers and
other technology?

What are schools offering their parents and pupils? Over the last
decade we have seen an increasing awareness of the importance of
managing the school's reputation, or marketing. The pressure to
define precisely what a school is offering and to communicate it
to the customers can be seen to be increasing. Differentiating a
common product and finding a niche in their locality will be seen
to be an increasing management trend for schools.

Change

Change has become normal and persistent. We have come out of
an age in which change took place and then we were on a plateau
and nothing changed again for a while. Now constant change and,
indeed, increasingly rapid change can be seen to be the norm. The
key points to consider are:

● change has become pervasive, persistent and normal;
● there is an accelerating rate of technological advance;

- the business cycle and the economic cycle are no longer predictable and thus the nature of work, the economy and employment
  in the future are also uncertain;
- all products have shorter life-cycles reducing from years to
  months in some cases, e.g. computers, cars, insurance.

One of the big myths in education is that the changes following
the 1988 Education Reform Act have worked their way through the
system and that we are now in a stable pattern for the next few
years. It would seem that the expectations of customers, the nature
of competition and the ongoing rate of change itself is unlikely
to leave education in a backwater. Education is at the forefront
of society's attempts to come to terms with this new reality. It
is difficult to imagine that education and the nature of schooling
will not itself have to change radically.

Reengineering: three concepts and one outcome

The definition outlined earlier stated that reengineering was 'the
fundamental rethinking and *radical redesign* of *business processes* to
achieve *dramatic* improvement in critical contemporary measures
of performance, such as cost, quality, service and speed'. If we are
to encompass a reengineering approach to designing an effective
primary school in the year 2000, then an examination of these key
concepts is necessary.

Fundamental rethinking

Instead of thinking about how we can get the most out of existing
structures and resources, what is needed is *breakthrough* thinking.
We are all told many times 'I would like to do that but we don't
have the resources'. That's because either the speaker is waiting
for a fairy godmother (or should it be godperson?) to wave a magic
wand to get more resources and will do nothing until that happens
or that he/she is incapable of rethinking how to tackle a particular
challenge. A reengineering approach would suggest that some basic
questions are asked:

- why do we do what we do?
- what do customers (pupils) really need?
- does what we do contribute significant 'added value' to the
  education product?

We should be ignoring the *what is* and concentrating on the
what should be framework for analysis. It could be considered as

planning backwards: what are the outcomes which we want? We must focus on what we must do as a school before we come to worry about how to do it. Then we have to think differently about how to do it. We cannot significantly improve the quality of our school by simply working harder. We have to work smarter not harder, and the smarter involves not slicker ways of doing the same things but fundamentally different ways of doing those things. A useful saying to remember is 'sacred cows make the best burgers'. All organisations have things that they believe have to be done in certain ways or cannot be changed and it is by fundamentally rethinking those core factors that we are likely to achieve breakthrough thinking. Do teachers contribute to pupils' learning? The answer would obviously seem to be yes. But the most common assumption that follows is one that more teachers increase learning. As was suggested earlier in this chapter, within certain financial parameters fundamental questions about the mix of resources between teachers, para-professionals, technology, learning resources, the peer group and the parental and wider community may suggest fundamentally different resource mixes (class size for example) than those that predominate at present.

Radical redesign

This involves the avoidance of superficial changes and getting to the root of the problem. It is about disregarding existing structures and processes and being involved in re-invention rather than incremental adjustment. The message for those adopting a reengineering perspective must be to start from scratch, put everything on the table and allow no 'sacred cows' that cannot be touched. In Australia I visited Methodist Ladies College. This is an independent girls school for pupils aged 5–19. In the junior school the head of primary, Pam Dettman, was faced, on appointment four years ago, with the challenge of how to provide the 450 girls with an effective approach to computer-aided learning and development. The incremental approach would have been to consider options like marginally increasing the number of computers in each classroom or setting up some sort of central facility. Instead she undertook a radical redesign of computers in education. After considerable research and consultations she put forward the recommendation that the school should take a far more radical approach than other schools in this area. If pupils were to see computers as an integrated part of learning and as a tool to be used at home or at school as an individual productivity and learning device, then each pupil needed her own notebook or lap-top computer. The school adopted the policy that part of the fees which it charged for each pupil would be required to purchase a notebook computer. On my visit 5 year old pupils were putting their lunch boxes in a locker in one corner of the room and their computers on charge in another when they came into class in the morning.

Readers will immediately say that that is fine for private schools but that the state sector doesn't have those resources. However, resources are also difficult in the private sector, but that is not the point. Pam Dettman started by radically redesigning her problem, not by limiting her management imagination to current thinking or current orthodoxy. A school with 11 teachers all with 28 pupils in a class could be reorganised into 10 classes of 30 pupils and could release enough money to buy thirty lap-top computers each year!

Business processes

Business processes can very simply be considered as 'the way that work gets done'. How do schools deal with pupils? There are staff with management responsibility, staff with teaching responsibility, administrative staff in the office, caretakers and cleaning staff with responsibility for the school fabric and governors and parents who also link into the process. But do we consider how we operate an effective system without harmful demarcation and duplication of effort that wastes time and confuses the pupil or parent who sees the school as a single entity?

What is needed is a review of key factors that impact on the processes of the school:

- organisation structures;
- management practices;
- staff working practices;
- culture of the organisation;
- values of the organisation;
- the interface between governors, headteacher and staff — working towards the same ends?

The core business process of an organisation can be considered to be a cross-functional collection of activities that together produce a meaningful outcome for a customer. How do we in schools produce meaningful outcomes for our pupils? How can we ensure that every child leaving primary school has adequate reading skills — indeed how can we prevent pupils leaving the education system functionally illiterate? If we are to improve significantly educational outcomes, it is vitally important that we focus on the core business process and on the way that we harness the variety of people, resources and structures to that end.

Dramatic improvement

The earlier definition of reengineering stated that its goal was to achieve a '*dramatic* improvement in critical contemporary measures of performance, such as cost, quality, service and speed'. While the main focus of education should be in the achievement of a dramatic improvement in the quality of education as measured by pupil outcomes, we should not ignore the cost and service elements.

In quality terms there has been a vast improvement in the reliability and quality of consumer goods over the last 20 years, spearheaded by Japanese manufacturers. We now expect new cars to be perfect and not to have to return them for initial faults to be corrected. Yet in education, HMI reports on primary schools for a considerable period of time have stated that 25 per cent of lessons seen were less than satisfactory. We may have abolished what was known as the 'Friday car' but the 'Friday lesson' is still with us! We need a dramatic improvement in standards to achieve quality with our present outcome measures, let alone with the standards which we will need to achieve in order to meet the education demands of the next millennium. Thus, performance improvements to meet the challenge of the future will truly have to be dramatic.

The improvements required in the cost and service outcome elements are also considerable. The level of consumer expectations and competition in education, as in other fields, means that increasing emphasis will have to be paid to improving the service which schools provide to their customers. Re-engineering means getting more from less. It is likely that the resource framework will need to demonstrate how schools can achieve higher outputs from less resources. In this framework, the key processes in the business reengineering movement will play a vital part.

The need to change the nature and dimensions of leadership and management in primary schools

Management and leadership in all organisations can be seen to be shifting from structures where managers saw organisations as hierarchical pyramids, where:

* workers did specific tasks;
* managers acted as controllers and planners;
* managers saw themselves as motivators of staff;

to ones where new roles for management are emerging. During the 1980s and early 1990s a number of reactions and stratagems have become apparent in both the public and private sector of which the following provide an example:

- Downsize   — divest products/services;
                  — cut labour costs;
- Casualise labour — make part-time;
                  — de-regulate;
                  — make short-term contracts;
- De-centralise   — empower sub-units;
- De-layer   — flatten the structure.

The way that managers and leaders need to operate in these new structures can be seen in Figure 9.2.

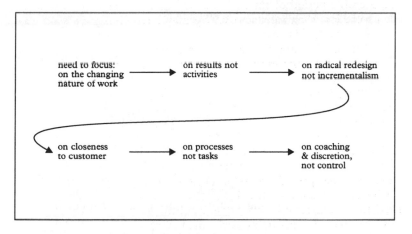

Figure 9.2   Realisation of new ways forward

The move to the manager as coach and facilitator

In this increasingly complex and rapidly changing environment, managing through others, not by direction but by coaching and supporting, is seen as the most effective management approach for the 1990s. Coaching is defined by Kinlaw (1989, p.31) as 'a mutual conversation between manager and employee that follows a predictable process and leads to superior performance, commitment to sustained improvement, and positive relationships'. The main features of coaching are that:

- it is an ongoing process;
- it is aimed at sustaining improved performance;
- it can be for groups not just individuals;

- it develops positive relationships so that the participants work together effectively in the future;
- it gives or invests continuing authority and responsibility and resources to people but within boundaries and with the manager still ultimately accountable;
- it is committed to valuing and developing people in their current and future careers.

Criteria for a management model of coaching

To enable coaching to take place and be effective certain criteria must be present. Coaching:

- must enable two-way respect;
- must be disciplined and systematic;
- must be predictable and user friendly;
- must be able to be used again and again;
- must allow the manager to counsel, mentor, tutor and confront members of the team;
- must lead to solutions and positive results.

Developing a 'management by coaching' culture

If we are to build successful schools by empowering others, then the organisation must be open and clear to everybody about values, aims and vision. It must focus on giving people competence: enabling them to learn; giving them the skills so that they feel they that can do their work; and making a public commitment to supporting them in this way. It is important that the people in the organisation can see that they can influence innovations and plans and contribute to problem solution. To do this, management must cope with its own apprehensions about giving up the traditional functions of planning, organising, directing and controlling. It can best do this by 'setting the big picture' so that everyone is clear about the context in which they are operating.

Conclusion

Where does this leave the manager and leader of a primary school facing the challenge of taking his/her school into the next century and millennium? The answer is probably to develop the characteristics of a radical thinker and a management coach.

The radical thinker needs to accept that the three Cs of customer expectations, competition and change are altering so rapidly that incremental quality improvements are unlikely to prove adequate to the task. It seems fairly obvious that a prerequisite for operating a successful educational institution is that it should offer quality to its clients. Indeed when planning for the year 2000, quality is an absolute minimum. But, there we have it: it is a minimum and not a solution. The reengineering movement offers us some clues. The economic system and the framework in which we operate are changing in such a fundamental way that incremental improvements no longer will be adequate.

Managers must have the vision to empower a flexible and responsive workforce. Often one person's decentralisation has become another person's centralisation and the opportunity to rethink has been lost. If we believe in decentralisation to organisations do we believe in decentralisation within organisations? Can we, in this new dynamic educational environment, decentralise decision-making to the educationalist interacting with the pupil so that information, knowledge, power and rewards lie at that level rather than at the top of the hierarchy? This means giving effective resource power, once the strategic dimensions have been set, to much smaller groups in organisations. However, giving power is not in itself enough. The sub-units need to be given information and knowledge to be in the same position as managers at the senior or strategic levels in the organisation so as to be able to make effective decisions. Control over information is linked to power and therefore disseminating information and knowledge is very challenging to those in traditionally structured hierarchical organisations as it threatens their power base. In this context thinking of the manager as coach may be the appropriate metaphor for the future.

What we need is leaders of educational institutions with vision, rather than those who say 'if it ain't broke don't fix it'. The reply we probably need is 'if it ain't broke you haven't looked hard enough' or 'if it ain't broke — break it'. We need radically new ways of thinking about how we lead and manage in the 21st Century.

References

Beare, H. and Slaughter, R. (1993) *Education for the Twenty First Century* Routledge.

Davies, B. (1994) 'TQM — a theory whose time has come and gone' *Management in Education* 8, No. 1, Spring 1994.

Hammer, M. and Champy, J. (1993) *Reengineering the Corporation* New York: Harper Collins

Kinlaw, D.C. (1989) *Coaching for Commitment* Pfeiffer.

Index